TAROT
FOR
TEENS

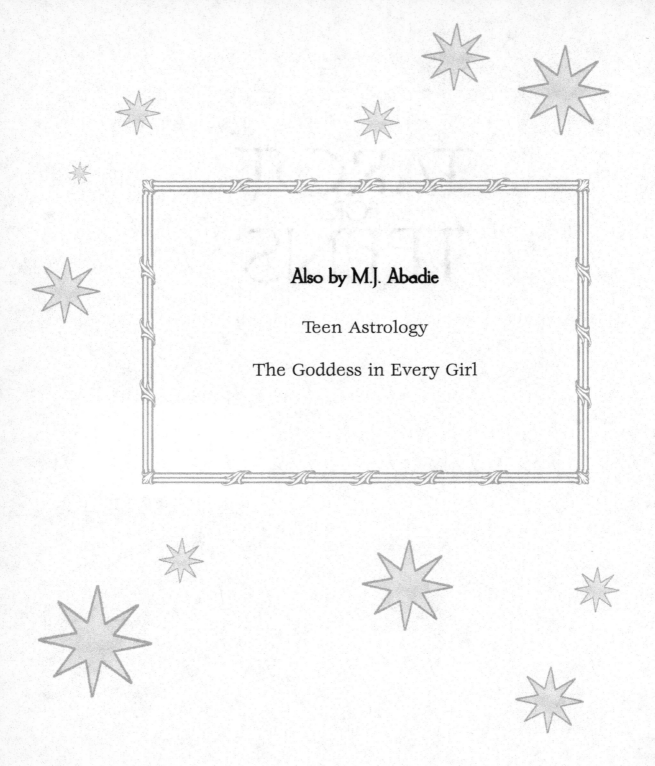

Also by M.J. Abadie

Teen Astrology

The Goddess in Every Girl

TAROT FOR TEENS

M. J. ABADIE

Bindu Books

Rochester, Vermont

Bindu Books
One Park Street
Rochester, Vermont 05767
www.InnerTraditions.com

Bindu Books is a division of Inner Traditions International

Library of Congress Cataloging-in-Publication Data

Abadie, M. J. (Marie-Jeanne)
  Tarot for teens / M.J. Abadie.
      v. cm.
Contents: Getting to know the tarot — The art of interpretation —
Preliminaries to reading — The major arcana and their meanings —
More about the trumps — Interpreting the major arcana in a reading
— The minor arcana — Interpreting the minor arcana — The wands —
The pentacles — The swords — The cups — Spreads for readings.
  ISBN 978-0-89281-917-1
  1. Tarot—Juvenile literature. [1. Tarot.] I. Title.
  BF1879.T2 A28 2002
  133.3'2424—dc21

                                        2002010235

Printed in the United States

10   9

Text design by Mary Anne Hurhula
This book was typeset in Veljovic, with Ashley and Carlton as display
typefaces

Contents

Acknowledgments

My thanks go first to Laura Schlivek, my project editor at Inner Traditions/Bindu Books. As always, our collaboration on this project has been a pleasure. I would also like to thank acquisitions editor Jon Graham for his enthusiasm and support, Victoria Sant'Ambrogio for copyediting the book, Mary Anne Hurhula for creating the attractive interior design, and Peri Champine for designing the delightful cover. Thanks, too, to Tom Juvan for his good page-layout suggestions and his careful proofreader's eye. Last, but certainly not least, the support of the publisher, Ehud Sperling, has been invaluable.

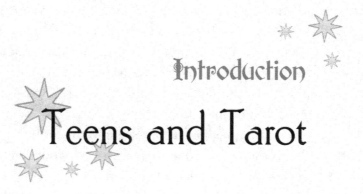

Teens and Tarot

*However we choose to define psychic
for ourselves, we must do so from a perspective of the whole human being acting in
interaction with a holistic universe where anything is possible. We have only to open
our minds and release our fears to summon
marvelous genii capable of astounding feats
from the depths of our own psyches.*
M. J. Abadie, Your Psychic Potential

What is the Tarot and why should teens be interested in it?

Simply put, the Tarot is a system of *divination* that goes back
hundreds—perhaps thousands—of years. Its use has been recorded
during many historical periods, and it was especially popular during the Middle Ages. A system of cards, consisting of seventy-
eight individual cards, it is known as an "occult" tool. The word
occult simply means "hidden" and has no negative meanings.

In our ever more complex world, teens daily face challenges

"We know that the core of the neuroses of our time is the religious problem, or, stated in more universal terms, *the search for the self*. In this sense, neuroses, like the mass phenomena resulting from this situation, are a kind of sacred disease."

Erich Neumann,
Art and the Creative Unconscious

"*Search* is an expression of the urge to discover what 'holds the world together at its inmost core' (Goethe, *Faust*) to establish an order and meaning for our place in the cosmos. Man's thrust into outer space is the counterpart of the quest into inner space in search of integration and fulfillment."

Edward C. Whitmont, M.D.,
The Return of the Goddess

unknown in the past. Thus, many are turning to various forms of divination, including the Tarot, astrology, the *I Ching,* and runes.

The Tarot is especially popular with teens these days, especially now that a large variety of attractive decks are available, using themes as diverse as Native American, fairy-tale symbolism, and the Goddess. The Tarot can give teens a big-picture snapshot of their lives at any given moment, as well as answer pertinent questions about specific concerns.

Although various means of divination have been used for fortune-telling—that is, predicting the future—the primary purpose of the Tarot (and other systems as well) is to tap into the inner wisdom we all possess.

All these systems have in common the same purpose: to find out where one is in one's own particular universe and to get a handle on what's going on *inside oneself.* So often we are confused—and teens are especially susceptible to confusion both from almost always being in a heightened state of emotions, as well as from sheer lack of experience.

However, it's important to realize that none of these systems should be used to predict the future, for none of us can do that with certainty. We are not passive spectators in our own lives— we are active participants. Tarot cards show what *energies* are in play at the time of the reading. As the entire universe, including our personal one, is always in flux, these energies are not stagnant or static but are in constant motion. What's true today may no longer be true tomorrow or next month.

Generally speaking, depending on the depth of the Tarot reading and what it reveals about the question being asked, the information given in a reading lasts for only a few days or weeks. Thus, you should use Tarot readings carefully and continually, and not base any major life decisions on a single reading.

How the Tarot Works

The universal significance of the Tarot is thought to spring from the *anima mundi*, or soul of the world. This source of knowledge is like a cosmic library filled with the accumulated wisdom of the entire human race, which we can all tap into through the symbolism of the Tarot cards. Within this collective pool are all the basic figures found in religions, myths, legends, and fairy tales. These archetypal figures, with their magical storehouse of profound esoteric knowledge, are already embedded in our collective unconscious. This is why contact with these images in a reading or in contemplation and study of the cards allows their hidden counterparts—from the deepest layer of human collectivity—to become conscious forces that we can use to answer our questions and better our lives.

Tarot cards are wonderful for meditation. They act to stimulate the intuition, which is the gateway of the unconscious. They illuminate the hidden factors in our lives, of which often we are not aware. Yet these inner issues are secretly shaping the course of life. The Tarot, properly used, reveals them.

The pictures and symbols that appear on the Tarot cards, especially in the "trump" cards known as the Major Arcana—the twenty-two primary picture cards of the deck—relate directly to fundamental human psychological and spiritual experiences. The study and practice of Tarot puts a person in touch with deep inner life, and the deeper he or she goes, the greater the understanding. While it is true that Tarot can be used to help answer everyday questions and to address immediate problems, its true use is for *spiritual development and the discovery of the Self*.

"Symbol is myth's vehicle, the chariot by which legend and story, and myth's higher form, religion, is drawn through the heart and mind, and through time, the pages of history. Symbols express underlying patterns of thought and feeling stemming from the mythological roots that still affect us in a very real way."

M. J. Abadie,
Awaken to Your Spiritual Self

Though we may never know the true history of the Tarot for sure, what we do know is that we are free to use the cards and the wisdom they contain to solve problems, make our lives more understandable, and further our spiritual development. The Tarot cards tell a powerful story of the development of human life. It is a universal adventure story, which each one of us undertakes in his or her own way, using the symbols that are presented at the moment of a reading. Its amazing flexibility has enabled the Tarot and its revealing symbols to last through long and tumultuous centuries and still be relevant to us today.

The Structure of the Tarot

A tarot deck consists of seventy-eight cards. They are divided as follows: The Major Arcana consist of twenty-two cards, also called *trumps*. The Minor Arcana consist of sixteen court cards, which are similar to modern playing cards and include a King, Queen, Knight, and Page; and forty number cards known as *pip* cards.

The Major Arcana cards are the most important: they reflect the spiritual journey of all humanity, from newborn innocence to self-actualization in the world. Also, as far as we know they are the oldest. The court cards and the number cards seem to have been added at a later date, probably in the fourteenth century. Apparently, these cards were derived from a popular Italian card game called tarrochi.

Again bearing a resemblance to modern playing cards, the court cards and the pip cards are divided into four suits—Wands, Pentacles, Swords, and Cups. The court cards can refer to people in our lives or to aspects of ourselves. Often in teen readings the court cards—especially the Kings and Queens—relate to significant adults with whom the teen is dealing, such as parents, teachers, and other authority figures. They signify the entire web of relationships. In addition, some court cards, especially the Knights and Pages, can indicate external events or inner conditions.

There are ten pip cards in each suit—forty cards in all. These number cards refer to all the stuff of daily life, our everyday concerns, events, reactions, behaviors. In addition, the pip cards have numerological significance, which we will discuss later.

Understanding Archetypal Symbolism

As the Major Arcana cards are based on archetypal symbolism, a basic understanding of the way that archetypes work will help you interpret the cards more fully. An archetype is an inward image that functions in the human psyche. It is a product of our own intuitive self—something we know about deep inside, even if we aren't conscious of knowing it. Archetypes are common to all of humanity. For example, we all have an image of a Mother figure inside ourselves, even if a real mother has been missing in our life. When viewing the world from an archetypal perspective, it's important to remember that all visible forms are connected to and supported by underlying archetypal principles, which are universal. These reflect both our inner and outer experience. A brief list follows, detailing the archetypal worldview.

- The world is considered a reflection of the greater whole of the Universe, or the Divine Mind, which both interacts with and transcends material reality.

- Everything is part of the greater whole, which has order and design. Nothing happens by coincidence and there are no truly random events. What appears to be chance is a clue to the overall pattern of meaningfulness in life.

- Reality is multi-dimensional. There are phenomena of which we are usually unaware, but everything is connected at some level, both the visible and the invisible worlds.

- The processes of cyclic change are part and parcel of everyone and everything; all arises, grows, and decays.

- In addition to supporting visible forms, archetypes are also an expression of subtle mathematical or geometrical principles and patterns, as shown by astrological concepts and other forms of divination using numerology, including the Tarot.

The Spiritual Journey through the Major Arcana

The twenty-two Major Arcana trump cards represent a path to spiritual enlightenment through the use of archetypal symbols. Beginning with the Fool, who has no number but is represented by zero, the seeker follows the cards in successive stages of development until he or she reaches card number twenty-one, the World. Used as a tool for spiritual development, each card has a particular significance, and each represents both internal states and external situations that have deep personal significance.

Now we will take a brief look at the Fool's journey through the Tarot Major Arcana. It's important to know that we *all* come into the world as the Fool—that is, we are newborn, fearless, and ready to learn the lessons life has to teach us. The Fool is always shown as a carefree youth, looking upward, in motion, and about to step off a cliff into thin air, trusting in the Universe to support his actions. Although usually depicted as a young man, the Fool can represent either sex.

Trump O—The Fool

This is the beginning of the journey that is a life. At this stage, the person is innocent and trusting. The Fool is free of guile and worry. Fresh-faced and adventurous, the Fool looks toward the sky, not down at his feet. Although he teeters on the edge of a precipice, he remains totally unaware of danger. Often he is accompanied by a little dog. Dogs symbolize the ability to follow an invisible trail: they are psychic creatures. The Fool represents our own free-spirited self before it got bogged down in daily life. Fortunately, we can always return to that state when the Fool turns up in a reading.

Trump I—The Magician

The Magician is indeed a magical card. He is usually shown with the tools of his trade laid out before him on a table. It is his job to teach the Fool to use the creative energy of the Universe, and the appropriate tools and instruments, in order to shape a life full of purpose and creativity. The Magician understands how the world works—not the ordinary world we see around us dimly, but the energies that stand behind the workings of the Universe. The Magician indicates your latent abilities to use logic, consciousness, awareness, objectivity, and energy to make your life work.

Trump II—The High Priestess

This is a card of mystery and depth. While the Magician is about using *mental* abilities to bring about manifestation of our wishes and desires, the High Priestess is about the nonmaterial realm. She represents the hidden, spiritual, inner Self with all of its unseen processes, such as intuition, moods, emotions, and reactions that may seem illogical but that stem from our inner knowings. She is the ruler of Night and all the unfathomable aspects of the Universe of which we are only dimly aware and cannot reach with the logical mind alone. When the High Priestess appears, it is a message to look inside yourself for guidance.

Trump III—The Empress

The Empress is a figure related to the Great Goddess of antiquity. She is Mother in the universal sense. Having encountered both the outer and inner worlds of being, the Fool now meets with the archetypal Mother. Often called the "marriage card," when the Empress appears in a reading for a teen she indicates that marriage is an issue in the teen's life. This does not usually mean you are actually going to get married (considering your age, of course) but it can indicate that the *meaning* of marriage may be a preoccupation. It can also mean a marriage in the family, or a pregnancy, for the Empress represents fertility and maternal nourishment.

Trump IV—The Emperor

It is interesting that the Emperor, who is the male counterpart of the Empress, *follows* her. This would indicate that the maternal principle comes before the paternal principle. The Emperor is very much of this world, representing authority, control, rationality, power, and dominion over others. The Emperor is about worldly concerns and often represents teens' needs to master life on the material plane. The Emperor can also advise of problems with authority (depending on where the card falls in the layout) or a need to develop your own power.

Trump V—The Hierophant

The Hierophant is a figure who teaches the Fool about institutional realities such as church and state. He is a symbol of the status quo, of what is already established in terms of traditional values and moral requirements. Also known as the Pope, the Hierophant signifies all that is conservative and orthodox. He is opposed to change and enforces the social codes of the society. In a reading for you as a teen, the Hierophant (depending on his place in the layout) shows that dealing with what is already in place is an issue—sometimes a difficult one.

Trump VI—The Lovers

Having traversed the mental and intuitive aspects of life, having met the basic female and male principles, and having dealt with worldly necessities, the Fool is now ready to confront the issue of love. But not necessarily the idea of being *in* love. What the Lovers card portrays is the awareness of the Other, or dualism. Love is a difficult matter and the younger you are the more difficult it can be. When the Lovers card turns up in a reading for a teen, it is a warning about making choices. The choices you make now will affect you the rest of your life, whether or not they are choices about romance. The Lovers card does not necessarily denote a romantic relationship, but it does indicate the need to think carefully about all your relationships: friendships, romantic desires, sexuality, what attracts you and why. An important card, the Lovers often turns up when you need to make an important choice.

Trump VII—The Chariot

Having reached the Chariot, the Fool is now faced with the challenge of making the many dualities in life go smoothly together. Usually pictured as a military man driving a chariot with one black and one white horse, this card speaks to the need to reconcile opposites, whether the opposing tendencies are in ourselves or in the external world. The Chariot teaches that life involves both conflict and resolution, usually through compromise. In a teen reading, the Chariot will show a need to deal with and balance opposing forces. For example, if your parents were going through a divorce, the Chariot might appear, challenging you to run a steady course in the face of difficult times. Whatever issue you are facing, when you see the Chariot in a reading, it means you are required to do a balancing act.

Trump VIII—Strength

Strength is a wonderful card. Often shown as a woman opening the jaws of a lion, or cuddled up with the king of the jungle, Strength is about the Fool's need to develop self-confidence and self-esteem, leading to inner strength. In a girl teen's reading, Strength often signifies that she is coming into her own, sometimes after a period of trial, for Strength is almost always a feminine figure. This card applies somewhat differently to a boy teen, where it can mean that physical strength isn't the only kind and that he needs to consider and develop inner strength.

Trump IX—The Hermit

The Hermit is a powerful figure. Often shown as an old man holding a lantern aloft, he represents guidance from the "other side"—or the need for such guidance. The Hermit teaches the Fool that there are powerful forces behind our visible world. In order to contact these forces, one must learn to meditate and to trust inner guidance, which is always available when one seeks it. As with all the cards, the position of the Hermit influences his message; but in a layout for a teen, he might call for a cessation of activities and a period of withdrawal into silence in order to meet the "guide within" and take advantage of the wisdom there. The Hermit may appear in a teen layout when there is turmoil in life, or when things don't seem to make much sense. Often the Hermit appears when you are overloaded with outside activities and need to spend time alone to sort things out and get them into a proper perspective.

Trump X—The Wheel of Fortune

This card suggests that the Fool is not in control of what goes on in the universe, or even in his own personal world. It shows that there are powerful forces operating that may seem random and unpredictable, but actually are part of an overall pattern of life. The Wheel of Fortune is not a negative card. It declares that by our previous decisions, choices, and actions we have put something into motion that cannot now be halted. In a teen reading, the Wheel of Fortune is an indication that taking everything for granted is not a good idea. It is a sign that you must learn this lesson: What you sow will be what you reap later on.

Trump XI—Justice

Having learned that there are forces beyond our control, when the Fool meets with Justice he is given to understand that despite the seeming randomness of life, certain patterns do exist, and our actions have measurable consequences. Justice turns up in a teen reading when there is a need for balance and harmony. For example, perhaps you were involved in a fight or a disagreement, and now you feel unfairly treated; but in order to set things right, you, too, must act justly. You know that life isn't necessarily fair—but it is important to take positive steps to ensure fairness in your own dealings with others.

"Abandon the search for God and the creation and other matters of a similar sort. Look for him by taking yourself as the starting point. Learn who it is within you who makes everything his own and says, 'My God, my mind, my thought, my soul, my body.' Learn the sources of sorrow, joy, love, hate. . . . If you carefully investigate these matters you will find Him in yourself."

Monoimus,
Gnostic teacher

Trump XII—The Hanged Man

Now that the Fool has learned the previous lessons, he needs to learn to let go and perhaps begin again. The Hanged Man is usually shown upside down on a tree limb, with one leg crossed over the other. Oddly, he doesn't look at all uncomfortable as he contemplates the universe from this position. In fact, he looks downright cheerful and optimistic! This interesting and intriguing card often indicates the possibility of taking an entirely new view of your life, of seeking new, unthought-of perspectives. In a teen reading, the Hanged Man may appear after a period of being unhappy or unsettled; he may be requesting some new thoughts about the situation. Or, a teen may literally feel turned upside down by life. The idea here is to abandon old ideas and to develop new ones more suitable to your spiritual development. It is a call to question materialistic values.

Trump XIII—Death

This card often frightens people when it turns up in readings. However, Death is definitely not a negative card, and you should not interpret it literally as meaning you or someone you love or know is going to die. What the Death card indicates is that something or even someone you have outgrown needs to "die"—you need to let go. Death is about transition. You might be going from junior high to senior high, or from high school to college, and you have to leave behind an entire way of life. It's also about *transformation,* which can be scary. However, without necessary transformation we fall into ruts of our own making and go nowhere. When Death appears, it is a wake-up call and an indication of significant change coming—like it or not!

Trump XIV—Temperance

Temperance is a lovely card. It usually shows an angel with wings and a halo of light rays, pouring a liquid from one cup or vessel into another. The angel may be male, female, or androgynous. The vessels, one gold, the other silver, represent the continuous interplay of the spiritual and material worlds. Temperance is an indication that the Fool has been "tempered" by life and now understands the necessity of cooperation, balance, harmony, receptivity, and creativity. When Temperance shows up in a teen's reading, it suggests the need for developing these qualities, sometimes in response to an experience of chaos or uncertainty.

Trump XV—The Devil

The Devil is another card, like Death, that tends to make people uneasy, especially if they have been brought up to believe in literal devil. And it is true that this card can appear rather fierce, depending on the deck you are using. The Devil's true meaning has nothing to do with evil or punishment. He usually appears with chains, sometimes with human figures in chains. Readers often gasp in alarm at his appearance in a layout, fearing he will "get" them. However, the Devil card is only a sign that one is (or feels) trapped in an oppressive situation. Looked at closely, this is often one's own fault. In a reading for a teen, the appearance of the Devil can declare the need to break the chains that bind him or her in a situation. Often the culprits are ignorance, unruly emotions, obsessions, attachment to material goods, poor impulse control, and negative thinking. All these are correctable.

Trump XVI—The Tower

The Tower card is another one that tends to upset or frighten people. It usually shows a tall tower being struck by lightning; sometimes bodies are flying out the windows. Like other cards that signify change, the Tower appearing in a layout clearly announces that you need to change in order to grow. Usually, the Tower, means drastic change. In the reading of a teen, it might mean getting away from activities, people, and behaviors that are destructive to growth and development. Or it might reveal a need to face some hard truths about yourself and take the steps to correct a situation before it gets out of hand and blows up in your face. Think of the Tower card as a warning, and heed its message seriously.

Trump XVII—The Star

The Star is one of my personal favorites. Following the hard lessons of the past few cards, the Fool now sees the light at the end of the tunnel—if he has done his homework and learned his lessons well. This serene and happy card usually shows a naked female figure kneeling at the side of a pond or pool of water. She is in the midst of a beautiful pastoral setting. She holds two pitchers; from one she pours into the stream while from the second she pours onto the ground. A main star is usually surrounded by a multitude of smaller stars, most often seven (there are seven stars in the heavenly Pleiades). The essence of the Star is hope and optimism. Her nakedness is a symbol for unveiled Truth and purity. The waters she pours are the very Waters of Life, some of which are being returned to the Source, some of which are being used to give new life to the land. When the Star appears in your teen reading, it is a most happy card and usually a clue that your own star is on the rise, often after a period of difficulty that you have successfully overcome.

Trump XVIII—The Moon

The Moon can be a confusing card for those who don't fully understand the symbolism of the Moon. While it is true that we don't see as much by the light of the Moon as we do by the light of the Sun, we see *differently* by the Moon's lovely light. The Moon is a magical, mysterious card that tells the reader to pay attention to dreams and messages from the inner depths. Many decks show the Moon with two dogs baying at it, but remember: dogs are symbolic of the psychic realm. When the Moon appears in a teen's reading, it can mean that you need to attend to your inner Self and its messages. You may be suffering from moodiness, be spaced out, or just be in a dreamy state of mind. The Moon card is telling you to pay attention to your personal and emotional needs. Meditation and rest are recommended.

Trump XIX—The Sun

The Sun is a happy, brightly colored card, usually showing a small naked boy riding on a horse under a blazing sun. Some decks show more than one child, or a young couple holding hands. The Sun is a symbol of progress. After wandering in the uncharted regions of Night, the Fool is now brought out into the light of day, and all is happiness, promise, and radiance. When the Sun appears in a teen's reading, it is a sure sign that you are being newly invigorated, perhaps after a time of troubles and uncertainty. The Sun card says that pleasure is coming your way and that your conscious planning and individual efforts will be rewarded with success. You may take a vacation to a sunny spot.

Trump XX—Judgment

Now, having been awakened by the newly risen sun, the Fool hears the trumpet of Judgment calling him to his earthly task. This is a time of rebirth and rebuilding. Many decks show Judgment as a rather negative-looking card, based on Christian ideas of Judgment Day. But other cultures consider judgment to be a time of re-evaluating our lives. When Judgment turns up in a teen's reading, it is sure to be a time of healing and transformation. You may have been "asleep," or not paying attention to what was going on around you, and you either got into trouble or just feel blah. The Judgment card is a wake-up call to your higher Self.

Trump XXI—The World

Now we are at the end of the Major Arcana. The cycle is complete. Our Fool has traversed an entire lifetime's worth of learning and is now ready for what psychologists call "self-actualization." Most decks show the World as a naked female figure entwined in a long scarf and holding two double-pointed rods, one in each hand. She is encircled by a wreath made of vines, leaves, and flowers. The World card signifies the completion of the journey started by the Fool in his quest for spiritual enlightenment. When the World card turns up in a teen's reading, it tells that some process—inner or outer, or a combination of both—has been achieved. It could mean graduation from high school, acceptance at the college of your choice, getting a job, or selecting a career. Depending on the current situation, your question, and the position in the layout, the World card says you are getting what you have rightfully earned, with blessings aplenty.

The more you learn about the Tarot, the clearer it becomes that its motifs refer directly to fundamental human psychological and spiritual experiences. As you continue to study the cards and practice using them, the deeper your understanding grows, and the more they resonate to the inner life.

Choosing a Tarot Deck

As the saying goes, one picture is worth a thousand words. The illustrations on a deck of Tarot cards speak directly to the deepest level of our beings. Today we have dozens of card decks, some of ancient origin, some newly minted by those who are attempting to bring this wonderful system of self-development into current times, using modern images and themes such as Native American, feminist, ecological, and many, many others. A visit to a book-store or a meta-physical store will reveal the wide variety of Tarot decks now available.

In choosing a deck, especially if you are a beginner, go by the "feel" of it to you. This book is applicable to any and all Tarot decks with the standard seventy-eight-card structure described earlier.

Eventually, you may want to work with more than one deck, but it is best to start with only one for learning purposes. Then, once you are thoroughly familiar with the cards and their meanings, you can branch out and experiment with other decks.

The Rider-Waite-Smith Tarot Deck

During the nineteenth and early twentieth centuries, interest in occult disciplines, including astrology, the Tarot, ritual magic, the Hebrew Cabala, Gnosticism, and geomancy, grew to new heights. (This interest never waned and eventually led to the proliferation of designs of Tarot decks we see today.) A group called the Order of the Golden Dawn came into being and devoted itself to the renewal of "magical" studies and practices. Established around 1887, this group had as its members Samuel MacGregor Mathers, Aleister Crowley, Arthur Edward Waite, and Paul Foster Case, among others. These men were influential in their time and produced many writings. In 1910, Waite commissioned artist and dramatist Pamela Coleman Smith to illustrate a Tarot deck. This deck, published as The Pictorial Key to the Tarot, soon became quite famous. Symbolically influenced by a number of occult philosophies, this deck has had sustained popularity and is usually the first choice for the beginner. It's a good choice for teens just starting out, because it is basic, and because many interpretive books use its illustrations as the basis for their interpretations. The pictures illustrating each card in this book come from the Rider-Waite-Smith deck.

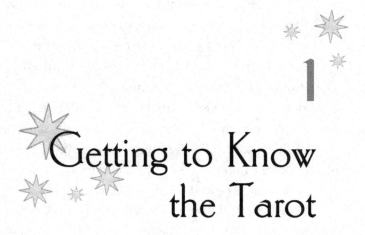

Getting to Know the Tarot

The Tarot is a powerful tool, and as with any power tool, you must use it with care and respect. It's not that the Tarot can hurt you like an improperly used electric saw; but in order for it to work, it is absolutely necessary not to be frivolous or have a shallow approach. The attitude with which you approach your Tarot readings will have a significant effect on their validity and usefulness, for the knowledge the Tarot contains connects with the deepest reaches of your psyche. You can use your Tarot deck to answer practical questions about your everyday concerns—school, tests, relationships with parents and friends, romance, money and work, or career and college issues—but its supreme value is in the development of your intuition, which in turn leads to spiritual development.

The word *psychic* puts some people off. It can cause conflicting and sometimes negative emotions, or fear of the unknown.

Many people think of psychic power as a dangerous force. This is nonsense. Everybody is psychic to one degree or another. It's like being musical or understanding mathematics or computers. Music notes may seem extremely mysterious if you can't read music. And certainly those unskilled in using computers find them awesome and sometimes frightening. (I speak from experience!) However, using psychic, intuitive methods is no more mysterious than working with computer language and programming. And unlike the ability to manipulate complex computer code, intuition is a built-in component of the human organism. Once you know the rules and are skilled at it, you realize it's been a part of you all along. Children, who have not learned to fear their natural abilities, often perform astonishing feats of intuition. They haven't been told it is "wrong" or "weird" to access intuitive knowledge directly, or to get information from a source other than the rational mind.

So, the first requirements of the novice Tarot student are to have an open mind toward the Tarot's power to provide information, to take what is given seriously, and never to attempt to manipulate people or events for personal gain. As in all of the arts—and divination is an art—talent is a factor; however, when learning any new skill, the more you work with it, the better you become. In other words, practice makes perfect—or at least it improves your performance.

Let's say you want information about the likely outcome of a major decision. You simply take out your Tarot cards and formulate your question, preferably in a special, private, quiet place. Before using your cards, take a few moments to relax completely, slowly allowing your conscious mind to let go of ordinary brain chatter, letting yourself sink to the deep level of your inner Self. Holding your cards, or shuffling them, concentrate on the situation troubling you, allowing it to become a part of your entire being. As you lay out your cards in a predetermined spread, allow yourself to be confident that you will get the right answer.

Believe that you already possess the ability to get answers and to understand what the cards are saying. When you do this, the Tarot then functions to focus the power of your intuition—a convenient way to get at the inner truth of the situation. In my experience, the Tarot often reaches right around surface problems to the real root of the problem. Put in psychological terms, it's common to displace the deeper problem with a simpler issue; but the cards will almost always point to what you might be hiding from yourself. They have an uncanny ability to get at the heart of the matter, often with surprising clarity. I've seen many examples of this in my Tarot reading practice.

Humans are only beginning to discover their almost unlimited intuitive capacities. One of France's most eminent brain specialists, Dr. Frederic Tilney, remarked bluntly, "We will, by conscious command, evolve cerebral centers which will permit us to use powers that we now are not even capable of imagining."

Being in touch with your psychic potential is a little like being an orchestra conductor and at the same time being all the instruments. Your conscious mind is the conductor, who must get everything going in concert. That includes both your "left brain," or rational mind, and your "right brain," or creative mind. (The right brain is the center of intuition and a host of other natural functions, some of which we are only dimly aware and don't understand very well, such as dreams.) In this task, the Tarot provides an excellent way of integrating all our seemingly separate parts.

When you first decide to do a Tarot layout, you automatically focus your conscious mind on the question and on the spread of cards, and this engages the intuition, providing clues to self-awareness. Because a Tarot reading is specific and detailed, it permits the left brain and the right brain to interact smoothly. Once you understand this process, you can tap into the cosmic reservoir for any purpose you wish. The Tarot deck puts this amazing power literally into your hands, acting as a catalyst to your intuition which then can produce information you need.

"The intuitive mind is a sacred gift and the rational mind is a faithful servant. We have created a society that honors the servant and has forgotten the gift."

Albert Einstein

Sally Gearhart, in *A Feminist Tarot*, says that it is easier to remember what the individual cards mean if we relate them to each other in groups.

I prefer to take them as a whole, but do whatever works for you. Everybody is different, nobody's memory works exactly like anyone else's. If splitting them up into smaller groups helps you to get at the meaning and retain it, by all means do so. The Major Arcana cards possess many different layers, and these layers reveal themselves gradually over time. It's like digging into an archeological site. There is the practical level—the Empress may refer to your mother or your wish to become a mother; there is the mundane, or worldly level—the Magician suggests you want to live a more creative life; then there is the spiritual level—the Devil may be telling you it's time for you to eliminate material concerns, which may be obstacles to your soul needs.

As you study the cards, respond directly to their images without letting your analytical, rational mind get in the way. Let your inner self tune into what you *feel*. Learn and use the interpretations here as a useful guideline, but remember they are not carved in stone. Feel free to be creative with your interpretations while remaining in the general ballpark of the information given here. These interpretations are a distillation of the understanding that has developed over centuries. Yet, as you will see when you get further along, there are many possible interpretations for each card, and many variables, depending on factors such as the placement of a card in the layout, the cards adjacent to it, and the general feel or tone of the layout. For example, a layout may look dark in color and yet have one or two brightly colored cards—perhaps the Sun, which would soften the darkness. Conversely, a layout might be generally positive and yet contain a negative card or two, coloring the total picture. With practice, you will become proficient at sensing which meaning is most fitting.

At first, you will want to look up the meanings of each card and then put all of them together into a reading. This takes study and practice. After many years of doing professional readings, I have learned that a spread acts as a *template*, or a field, through which information flows. Of course, this does not happen overnight. It's important to first learn the standard meanings of each card. Eventually you get the knack of seeing a wholeness in your spread.

A Closer Look at the Cards

The basic Tarot deck consists of seventy-eight cards. As you know, twenty-two of these are known as the Major Arcana. The term *arcana* is related to the word *arcane*, which means "mysteries" or "secrets." These secrets represent the unknown fathoms of the Universe that reflect Universal Law. For this reason, the Major Arcana are the most complex and form the backbone of the Tarot system. You will need to study these the most to understand their many layers of meaning.

No matter which deck you use, each of the Major Arcana cards is illustrated with meaningful symbols, similar in all decks though they differ thematically. Some decks reflect nature themes, or are related to a particular tradition such as Native American, Goddesses, the legend of King Arthur, Greek mythology, and too many more to name here. As you have already seen, each of the Major Arcana is titled and numbered from one to twenty-one, with the Fool being card zero.

The other fifty-six cards are called the Minor Arcana, because they contain information that is of a less important nature, with meanings more readily available to the average person. The Minor Arcana are divided into four suits, like a deck of ordinary playing cards. These are the Wands, the Pentacles, the Swords, and the Cups. (*Note:* Different writers give a different order to the suits. I always use this order—Wands, Pentacles, Swords, Cups—because that way the suits correspond to the astrological elements in *their* order: Fire, Earth, Air, Water.) Each suit of fourteen cards contains four court or "face" cards—King, Queen, Knight, and Page. (An ordinary playing deck has only three court cards—King, Queen, and Jack.) Each suit also has an Ace as the One card and the rest of the cards numbered Two through Ten.

The Minor Arcana give *immediate* information. Each of the suits represents a separate area of your activity and growth. These are:

  ❖ **WANDS** Mental activity, the outer world, work or career
  ❖ **PENTACLES** Money, security, the physical world
  ❖ **SWORDS** Self, obstacles one is facing, spiritual issues
  ❖ **CUPS** Emotions, love, romance, the unconscious

You are a unique person unfolding your personality and your inner Self according to your own particular blueprint. You can't hurry the process, for it insists on its own time schedule. There are cycles in life. These are the patterns built into your development.

The Tarot used regularly can reveal these and suggest new directions. Use the Major Arcana as a guide to explore universal concepts as they apply to where you are in your life at the present moment.

Learning Tarot by Self-Teaching

First, of course, you need to study the cards and their meanings. Second, you need to become familiar with the various spreads or layouts. There are several given in this book, and you can also develop your own for special questions or for any other reason. Finally, you must *practice*. Learning to use the Tarot successfully is just like learning any other skill: if you are serious about learning and using it, you must practice. The need for practice always reminds me of an old New York joke. A tourist, late for a musical concert and lost, rushes up to an old Jewish street peddler and cries with great urgency:

"Quick, tell me how I get to Carnegie Hall!"

The old man intones, *"Practice, practice, practice."*

How often and when you practice is up to you. My advice is to practice often. When I began my own serious study of interpretation, I spent the first hour of every day laying out the cards and recording my interpretations. Previously, I had studied them primarily for their symbolic art, concentrating on learning the symbolism only, with no intention of doing readings. This worked for me very well, for by the time I had decided to put my knowledge of the symbols to work doing readings, I was well prepared. However, you can learn the meanings little by little by daily (or frequent) practice. *Always* record your interpretations in your Tarot notebook, along with your question, the layout you used, and which cards were in which positions in the layout.

If you cannot spend the first hour of your day with your cards, set aside a specific time and stick with a schedule, just as you would do with your homework or work on any project. Naturally, as with a musical instrument, the more time you practice, the more expert you will become. If it suits your aims, you can concentrate on the interpretations and the sections related to the spreads and readings.

If, as I hope, you undertake study of the Tarot for its wisdom, then I recommend that you concentrate on each of the Major Arcana cards one at a time, in order. Read the interpretation for that card given here, compare it to its counterpart in your deck, and focus totally on the card until you have a feel for its energy. After you have finished the Major Arcana, turn to the Minor Arcana. Study the number cards of the four suits one at a time, as each suit covers a single area of life. Then go to the court cards—often used to represent people—King, Queen, Knight, Page. Become familiar with those images. When you have completed this process, you will be ready to do practice readings.

Another way to study is to simply start laying out cards and then look up the meanings of the cards you have before you. This process will gradually impress the meanings on your mind, especially if you write it all down in your notebook. However, if you want to do readings of a high quality, it's best to first become acquainted with the meanings of the card deck as a whole.

Clearly, your proficiency in using the Tarot will be a direct result of the amount of time and effort you put into studying and doing your own interpretations. You can combine short periods of regular practice with less frequent, longer practice sessions. Whichever method you choose, as you study the cards and begin to use them regularly, you will gain a gratifying appreciation of this wonderful wisdom source and what it is able to reveal about the human psyche.

"Few people realize that they are looking at the world of their own thoughts and the world of their own feelings."
Wallace Stevens,
The Necessary Angel

The Art of Interpretation

With so many Tarot card decks now available in such a wide variety of themes, interpretation becomes largely a matter of your own familiarity with the deck you choose. Many of today's decks come with a small booklet explaining the particular symbols of that deck. However, as all true Tarot decks are based on the same structure, you can apply the interpretations given in this book to any deck you choose. Begin by becoming familiar with your deck. Your first impressions of the cards are important, because when you look at the illustrations on different cards, they engage your intuition, that part of your mind that knows without active intellectual effort. This is what pictures do. And different people will react to different symbolic illustrations. Consider this book as a guideline, not a dogmatic text. The illustrations on your cards will resonate with you according to your individual temperament and your intention in learning and using the Tarot.

Keep in mind that the original Tarot cards were influenced by multiple cultures. Behind them stands a mystery. Your own reaction to the cards is unique, like your thumbprint; and as you progress in your study and practice, you will no doubt develop a keen sense of what seems right to you in any given situation. Since, however, there are standard interpretations that have stood the test of time, at first it is best to learn these. After you have learned and practiced with them, you can take off on your own, letting your intuition be your guide within the general set of applicable interpretations. Do what makes sense to you.

It is important to be comfortable with the symbols on your personal deck of cards. If the art is not meaningful to you, get another deck. It's vital that you feel in harmony with the cards you are using if they are to reach into your intuitive depths. You'll be more effective if you're using symbols you can relate to. How a card speaks to you, how you feel about its symbols, is what counts. So, the first step in learning to interpret is to find a deck with which you feel compatible and to make friends with it.

Understanding the Symbols of the Tarot

On each card of the Major Arcana, every symbolic detail is meaningful. Symbols act on different levels of the psyche. Therefore, you need to examine your cards carefully. The more attention you pay to the symbols, the more their meanings will sink into your unconscious. Don't forget, in interpreting the Tarot you are engaging your *intuition,* which is not a logical/rational activity. If you are accustomed to being mostly logical (as most of us are), this new activity may at first seem weird. You may experience odd and unfamiliar sensations. Don't let this frighten you. Your intuition cannot hurt you. If you experience any negative feelings, make notes of which cards, or which symbols, produce the discomfort. Negative information is only that—information. Information from the psyche is like a weather forecast: if the weather is going to be stormy, we can take precautions.

Intuition is holistic—it uses *all* of you—and this gives it its power. Your unconscious is a huge data bank of experiences of

"Thoughts without content are empty, intuitions without concepts are blind. The understanding can intuit nothing, the senses can think nothing. Only through their union can knowledge arise."

Immanuel Kant,
Critique of Pure Reason

which you are not even aware. Your intuition has the amazing ability to tap into this data bank and come up with creative combinations to help you with interpretations. Intuition is an innovator with great creative ability. Examine each card carefully, especially the details, until you get the feel of what each card means to you.

Your Tarot Notebook

Start a personal book of impressions with the title of a card at the top of each page. Each time you work with the card and record your impressions, date your entry. Your impressions will change and expand as the symbols reach deeper into your unconscious to reveal their many-faceted selves.

Begin with the cards of the Major Arcana, or trumps. As you know, these are the most important and symbolically complex; they are believed to contain disguised knowledge. Notice the main figures on the cards, examining their postures, positions of their hands and limbs (what we call body language) for significance. Pay attention to the minor figures—human, animal, or inanimate—that appear with them. Observe the background and the foreground; everything, however small, is symbolically meaningful. Give yourself time to get used to your impressions, and expect them to change as you become familiar with the cards over time. (Beginners usually interpret each separate card in a layout and then put together a reading from the individual cards. This is a fine way to start. With time and experience you'll get a sense of the whole at a first glance of a layout.)

A detailed record of your practice readings is the best tool you can have to keep up with what you are learning. You can return to it frequently to check your progress. Don't analyze your responses intellectually—just note down whatever rises to mind spontaneously. Write out any questions that present themselves for further study. By doing this you will be creating the

TEEN TAROT TIP

Choose one of the Major Arcana cards to accompany you throughout the day. Think about it's meaning, and look at it frequently under different circumstances to see how you relate to the images on the card as you make your daily choices and decisions. Record your experiences in your Tarot notebook.

"It is the function of creative people to perceive the relations between thoughts, or things, or forms of expression that may seem utterly different, and to be able to combine them into some new forms—the power to connect the seemingly unconnected."

William Plomer

building blocks for a complete course of self-instruction. You will be surprised indeed to discover how significant were your first impressions to your entire process of learning to interpret.

For a time during this early period, you will still want to refer to the interpretations of others—such as you find in this book—but eventually that won't be necessary. You'll have internalized the symbols and they will "speak" to you themselves, without the intervention of others' interpretations.

It's a bit like playing a musical score. First, you must learn what the composer wrote, and what he or she intended. Then, with much practice, you free yourself to give the music your own interpretative spin while honoring the basic meanings.

Tarot Play Exercise

A COLORING GAME

Here is an extremely good way to get to know your cards and their symbols. Photocopy your Major Arcana cards, enlarging them as you do, and then color in the illustrations—without referring to your deck. By doing this, you tap into your intuitive mind, which reveals your personal response to the symbols. What color, for example, does the High Priestess suggest to you?

You can, of course, use this same color play process with your Minor Arcana if they contain art images. However, keep in mind that although the number cards are often illustrated, their symbols are not standardized. Many decks depict the number cards only decoratively, without any symbols. The most important symbols are those of the Major Arcana cards. It is these you want to impress deeply upon your unconscious mind, where they will sink down and become a part of you. See pages 30–31 for the symbolic meanings of colors.

Color Symbolism

Paying attention to the colors of the illustrations on your deck, and the colors you spontaneously choose on your own, can be a useful way to understand the symbolism of the cards. Here is a brief list of colors and the meanings generally applied to them. Your own feelings about certain colors may differ. For example, yellow is about optimism; but you may not actually like yellow, for whatever reason. If you feel a color doesn't match up with the suggested meanings given here, let your own feelings be your guide. Nothing is set in stone!

BLACK: Black is actually the absence of light or color. It can be either "basic black" or the color of mourning. Black is a symbol of concentration, fixed purpose, and resolution. It is not always negative.

BLUE: There are many shades of blue, from baby blue to navy blue, so no one meaning can be assigned to blue. The lighter shades suggest tranquility, like a clear blue sky. Blue generally is about peace and serenity, relaxation, devotion, gentleness, and truth—as in "true blue." The darker shades of blue can invoke introspection, patience, conservatism, deep understanding, and sadness, as in "having the blues."

BLUE-GREEN, OR TURQUOISE: The color blue mixed with green changes the vibration to one of healing and soothing. This is a nature color, one that speaks to mystical unity with nature. Native Americans consider the turquoise stone to be sacred. It may induce visions.

BLUE-VIOLET, OR INDIGO: Blue mixed with violet gives various shades of purple, such as lavender on the light end and indigo on the dark end. These shades are very spiritual and are indicative of reflection and going within.

BROWN: Another nature color, brown comes in many shades. The lighter shades, such as tan and beige, are about simplicity and lack of ego or ostentation. The darker shades, from milk chocolate to deepest brown, are related to the power of Earth and suggest earthly rootedness, stability, and fondness for home and hearth.

GOLD: The metal of the Sun, gold reveals pride and self-confidence. It suggests power, radiance, charisma, creativity, and success. Gold is often related to power and material goods. It can also represent luck.

GREEN: The color of Nature in all its living glory, green is about life itself. It suggests freedom, youth, growth, fertility. Green is also the color of American money, "the greenback," and is connected to gain and wealth, opportunity, prosperity, financial security. In the Druid tradition, it is the color of esoteric knowledge.

ORANGE: Traditionally, orange is associated with the Sun and vitality, energy, self-motivation. A warm color, it suggests action and boldness, self-expression and creativity. Orange implies extroversion as opposed to introspection. The red-orange shades, such as tangerine, intensify the action quality of orange: assertiveness, competitiveness, enthusiasm, willfulness, forceful action.

PINK: The lighter shades of pink suggest delicate sensibilities and soft romantic feelings. Darker shades, such as various rose colors, intensify the romantic feelings. Pink signifies affection, love, good feelings about one's self and others. It evokes romantic imagination, inspiration, music. The pink-orange shades, such as peach, are about warmth and softness, with the addition of enthusiasm and energy. The pink-purple shades, like mauve, have the meanings of pink but are more subtle, or shy and less outgoing.

PURPLE: Once the color of royalty, purple is generally considered to be the color of spirituality, inspiration, the psychic senses, altered states of consciousness, and high creativity. It retains its association with power, authority, and high status ("wearing the purple") while also suggesting nobility, justice, tolerance, and respect for law.

RED: A primary color of life and energy—the color of blood—red is the highest vibration on the spectrum. It declares vitality, activity, anger, thirst for action, desire, passion, and sexuality. Red can also represent negative action or over-impulsiveness. Adding violet to red creates a shade with passion added to the mystical nature of purple. The darker shades of this mixture, such as maroon, combine sensitivity with sensuality, adding desire for the riches of life and a love of power and worldly possessions.

SILVER: The metal of the Moon, silver represents the lunar energies and the ethereal beauty of the moonlit night. It is about romance and the mysteries of love. It represents integrity—"a sterling character"—honesty, idealism, receptivity to the inner world's messages, and a fascination with Night.

WHITE: White is actually the combination of all colors together and thus it speaks of unity and harmony. It symbolizes purity (a white wedding) and peacefulness (a white flag). It calls up innocence, spiritual seeking, purification of all types, absence of negativity, and the desire for integration of all faculties—mind, body, heart, spirit.

YELLOW: The color of optimism, cheerfulness, good tidings, happiness, luck, and charm, yellow suggests confidence and spontaneity, intelligence, adventure, and the enjoyment of life's pleasures. Mixing yellow with green, as with lime, adds a calming effect, as green centers. Yellow-green shades emphasize the intellect and coolness of mind while retaining the quality of energy that likes a challenge.

Preliminaries to Reading

You have found a Tarot deck that you really like and have brought it home. You're beginning to make friends with the cards. But you still have questions: How should you handle your deck? Where will you keep it? What step comes next? Let's give these questions some answers.

HANDLING YOUR DECK

Before you use your Tarot deck, wash your hands thoroughly in warm water, preferably with a pure soap, such as castile. Dry them and lightly apply some greaseless lotion. Care for your hands well; they serve as the direct physical conduit for incoming information as you hold the cards.

Treat your Tarot deck with the same care you would any possession of great value. Don't ever just leave it lying around after you have finished a study session or a reading. Decide on where you are going to store your deck. Make a special place for it, and return it to its own place immediately after you have finished using it. Proper respect for your cards and the work you do with them is a vital component to success.

Blessing Your Cards

I find that performing a short blessing ceremony over my cards before each use enhances my ability to get good results from my interpretations. It's rather like saying "Grace" before meals. You can devise your own blessing, making it either very simple or more complex as you see fit. You may feel comfortable with a brief acknowledgment of the Higher Power that stands behind the cards and your use of them, or you may prefer to elaborate your blessing with a prayer or some other method of preparing yourself. A simple blessing ritual I often use is to just place the entire deck on the table and then hold my hands over it, palms down, and say, silently or out loud,

> I call upon the Higher Powers to bless and protect these cards as my intention
> is to use them for good only. I request that only good shall come from my use,
> and I declare any negativity will be turned away.

LEARNING TO SHUFFLE YOUR CARDS

As most Tarot decks are larger than a deck of ordinary playing cards, learning to shuffle them takes a bit of practice. You will need to break in a new deck, which is likely to be stiff and most probably protected by a coating that makes the cards slick. Ruffling the cards at the edges a few times will help to make them flexible. With handling and manipulation of each card separately, the deck will become softer and easier to shuffle.

Shuffling is a personal matter. It's important to get comfortable with shuffling your cards, whatever method you decide works best. You can shuffle—or mix—the cards in any manner that is comfortable for you. Some readers shuffle like professional gamblers, while others use gentle methods of mixing the cards into a different sequence. You can make small piles and then combine them, or you might enjoy putting them all out on a table and mixing them with your palms down. Be sure to keep the cards face down while shuffling or mixing. When reading for yourself or using the cards for practice layouts, you will want to shuffle them each time you use them.

Give some thought to how
you'd like to store your Tarot
deck. Most people I know like
to wrap their deck in a piece of
silk. Some use a pine box. I
don't recommend storing cards
in a leather pouch because
leather comes from a slaugh-
tered animal. Silk has calm and
soothing characteristics, but
any natural fabric will do.

The basic idea is to put
your cards in a protected place
and always keep them there. If
you use more than one deck
for different purposes, you
may want to store each deck
differently. Again, it's a matter
of personal choice.

If you read for others, you have the choice of shuffling the
cards yourself or allowing the person for whom you are reading to
do it. Some people don't allow anyone else to handle their cards.
Some, including myself, feel that the cards work best when the person being read for does the mixing. This is for you to decide. If you
want no one else to handle your deck, that is fine; but if you do
have the other person handle the cards to put his or her vibrations
into the deck, be sure to perform some kind of a clearing ritual
between uses. We'll consider clearing rituals in the next section.

When I do readings, I allow my clients the choice of how
they will handle the cards. If the person is shy or reluctant, I say,
"Just hold the entire deck in both hands for a moment or two
while you formulate clearly what you want the reading to
achieve." Then I do the shuffling.

A reader I know well shuffles the deck overhand precisely
seven times, not permitting his client to touch the cards at all.
With time and experience he has come to feel that this method
facilitates his ability to concentrate and "home in" on the totality
of the layout.

How you shuffle or mix the cards is related to your temperament. You may like to maintain complete control, or you
may enjoy having the other person take part in the process. You
don't have to stick with just one way. As you evolve in your use
of the Tarot, how you handle your deck will evolve too. You may
find that different methods are agreeable at different times. It's
good to remain flexible and not get into a fixed routine that might
clog up the flow of information from your intuition.

CLEARING VIBRATIONS

Clear the vibrations from your deck each time you use it, especially if you have read for another person. If you use a *different* deck
for private spiritual practice, you don't need to clear it of your own
vibrations; in fact, with use the deck becomes in tune with you. But

if you read for others with the same deck (which I do not advise) it's a good idea to clear it before each new reading. This also applies to the deck you use to do practice readings for yourself.

There are many methods of clearing, or purification. One is to simply say a short prayer over the cards and declare them free of all former vibrations and ready for the present intended use. Another—a Native American ritual—is to light some sage leaves and waft smoke over the cards. You can use one of the four elements for a clearing ritual, or you can invent your own ritual. As with blessing, this can be simple or elaborate. I use a simple method: I concentrate on clearing the cards as I slowly turn each one over onto the next through the entire deck. You will develop your own procedure. The idea is to put the vibrations of the moment into the cards, and clear them afterward. The important thing is not the actual ritual or method you use, but your intention to clear the cards.

Clearing with the Elements

FIRE Place your deck of cards in bright sunlight for an hour. Or light a candle where you consistently work and let it burn while you shuffle through the cards. Reserve a candle for this purpose, and extinguish it when you are done shuffling. Thank the Fire Spirit for its help.

EARTH Put your unwrapped deck into a shallow container. Cover the cards with a sheet of clean white paper. Pour salt over the paper and leave it for twenty minutes. Dispose of the salt by dissolving in water and pouring the salt water down the sink drain. Thank the Earth Spirit for its help.

AIR Gently fan your unwrapped deck with a folded piece of clean white paper or some feathers that are tied together (preferably gathered from the wild). You can also breathe gently on your deck while declaring your intention to clear. Thank the Air Spirit for its help.

WATER Water is an excellent element for clearing out any negative emotions. Invoke the Spirit of Water, ask it to cleanse and renew your cards, and spray-mist the air above. Or take a sprig from a plant, dip it into a pure water, and sprinkle the area where you use the cards. Thank the Water Spirit for its help.

RITUAL INTENTION

While the external form of a ritual is important, its real power lies in the *intention* you put into designing and using the ritual. A true ritual is more an internal than an external event. Ritual's outer form serves as a lens through which you are able to focus your psychic energy and the energy of the universe toward a specific purpose. Your state of awareness is what makes the ritual significant. Even though the actual form of the ritual itself possesses power simply because of the nature of the symbols being used, your *conscious intent* is what creates the desired effect.

Tarot Rituals

"The purpose of rituals is to help us focus on the issue or task at hand. Over the years, various people have discovered that certain action patterns help them to focus on the Tarot cards. They have systemized those patterns into rituals. Some of the most common rituals are:

> Keep your cards in a pine box
> Wrap your cards in silk (or cotton)
> Sleep with your cards under your pillow
> Never let anyone else touch your cards
> Lay all your readings out on a pine board
> Always face East when doing a reading
> Light a candle (or incense) for a reading
> Always face your reader
> Shuffle and cut three times to the left
> Shuffle once and cut three times
> Don't shuffle, cut once to the right
> Have only the readee shuffle
> Have only the reader shuffle

I feel that these rituals are very personal. . . . If you like rituals, use them. If you have developed a habit, like holding the remaining cards in your hand after dealing out the layout, and that habit seems to help you focus, use it. No ritual is especially sacred. Its value is that it helps you to focus on the reading. The most powerful rituals are often those we invent ourselves. Use whatever rituals feel right for you when working with the Tarot."

Gail Fairfield,
Choice-Centered Tarot

FORMULATING THE QUESTION

Before you do a reading, you must ask a question that you want answered. For practice readings, you may simply want to inquire about the circumstances of the present, unless you need advice about a specific situation or problem.

It's important to think about how you will phrase the question or questions. Clarity is vital. A murky or generalized question will produce a murky or unclear answer. For example, don't ask, "When will my life get better?" Instead, think through just what isn't working for you and formulate a question that is specific, such as, "How can I improve my relationship with my mother?"

If school is an issue, ask about a specific subject, test, or teacher. If friends are a problem, be clear about your thoughts. For example, "What is the true situation about _____ (fill in the name)?" If romance is on your mind, try asking something along the lines of, "What is the best course for me to follow in my relationship with _____ (fill in the name)?"

Other good questions to consider are, "Please show me the right steps to take next in my life," or, "Is there anything I need to know at this time?"

If you have a clear understanding of what you want the cards to tell you, you will get better results than if you generalize too much. However, it is always appropriate to ask for an overview reading of your life, because the cards will invariably point to any issues you might be denying, overlooking, or unaware of.

The type of question you ask will determine the layout you use. We'll discuss this further in Chapter 13, "Spreads for Readings." The more complex your question is, the more elaborate you will want to make the layout. For simple questions, simple layouts work best.

It's good practice to do frequent overview readings for yourself, recording them in your notebook for reference. Then, when

"The mind is restless, turbulent, obstinate, and very strong. To subdue it is more difficult than controlling the wind, but it is possible by constant practice and attachment. He who strives by right means is assured of success."

The Bhagavad Gita

doing a new reading, review the past readings so that you can compare them and judge your progress. Often, issues that you were concerned with a few weeks or even a few days earlier will have resolved themselves. If not, you can ask for additional advice concerning any lingering problems.

As life is in constant flux, readings don't last forever. Unlike your astrology chart, which is fixed at the moment of your birth, Tarot card readings tend to refer to the present state of affairs. I usually think of a reading as being good for about three months. This is because of the changing nature of things. For teenage readers, the changes can seem constant because their lives are still forming, and what may seem of utmost importance today is of no interest after a few weeks or months have passed.

This is especially true of romantic relationships—a subject that gives teens much anguish. The crush you are suffering over may well be replaced by a new focus of romantic interest quite soon. This is not to say that your emotions of the moment are not important, for they are. Whatever you feel, you feel intensely. I always take a teen's emotions extremely seriously, even if I know there is a likelihood they will change soon. Adults, too, go through emotional ups and downs, sometimes with even greater rapidity than do their teenage children! Always allow yourself to take yourself seriously; the Tarot will then reflect that attitude and give you useful information and advice. Consider it your friendly counselor, someone to whom you can always turn for true and sure help.

Learning to pose the right question in the right way takes practice—and patience—but it is well worth the effort in the end. It's better to avoid confusion and get it right the first time. Asking the right question seems to create an "energy zone" from which you can safely draw. This may be because when the question is just right, it seems to activate your intuition to focus sharply on the issue at hand, in an almost magical way. Sometimes, when

"Water is H$_2$O, hydrogen two parts, oxygen one, but there is also a third thing that makes it water and nobody knows what that is."

D. H. Lawrence

your question has been correctly framed, you will be positively astounded at the accuracy of the cards. I can't tell you exactly how this process works, but I know from experience that it does work. There are built-in connections between you and the Universe, and when your psyche gets involved, you automatically draw the cards you need.

Suppose you are trying to decide which college(s) to apply to. First you need to think about what you expect to get out of your college career. What are your aims? Are there financial issues? Do your parents favor one college over another for you? If you have a list of several colleges, you can ask a series of questions about each one. For example, say you are considering your state university and your local community college. You think State would be better, but your parents would prefer you to do your first two years at the community college nearby. You could start by asking the general question, "Is State the best place for me to go?"

The answer you interpret will determine your next question, perhaps "Will I be happiest at State?" "Is State the place where my degree will earn me the kind of job or career I want?" and so on. If you are determined to attend State, you might ask, "How can I overcome my parents' objections?" or "Are my parents right in wanting me to attend the community college?" You could also frame questions for the pros and cons of each college you are considering.

The same general approach should work for any long-term situation that you are facing. For less important everyday questions, devise simple, one-time queries. Say you are trying to decide between two different invitations to the prom. You might ask, "Will I have a good time with _____ (fill in the name)?" Or you may be considering joining a club or society. You could ask, "Will being a member of _____ benefit me?"

As you articulate the question in your mind while shuffling or mixing the cards, also be thinking about a suitable layout

"Shall I teach you what knowledge is? When you know a thing, to hold that you know it; and when you do not know a thing, to allow that you do not know it. This is knowledge."
Confucius

If, while you are shuffling your cards, one seems to leap out of the deck, pay attention to it. A card that asks for your attention in this manner is always important. Study it for meaning, then reinsert it into the deck at random and continue to shuffle.

(Chapter 13). Contemplate your question, or questions, from a relaxed frame of mind, and be ready to accept what the cards tell you. You will be surprised time after time. Often, even with a carefully thought-out question, what will surface are the underlying issues you are ignoring or unaware of. For instance, in the college example, the issue that surfaces may be your desire to defy your parents or to get away from them, even if you are not ready to go so far from home as the state university.

Be open to the answers the cards give you. If you are disappointed in the reading, wait a few days and then ask for clarification. When a reading points to a deeper issue than the one for which you have asked advice, it's important to pay attention. The Tarot cards have an uncanny ability to home in on the real situation. A question such as, "Will I get a date for the prom?" might be a reflection of insecurity about your attractiveness, and the cards may show this clearly. Remember that you can trust your cards because you can trust your intuition. However, never make any serious, life-changing decisions based on card readings. There are always too many variables and other factors involved in major life choices. Consider your readings to be guidelines, and don't ever do anything against your principles or your own common sense.

4

The Major Arcana and Their Meanings

The Major Arcana cards can be interpreted at many different levels. The more you study them, the more you will tap into their multilevel meanings and realize the almost endless subtlety they contain within their symbols.

In traditional societies, symbols were interpreted on three levels—personal, collective, and universal. At the personal level, the symbols pertained to the immediate situation of the individual. Naturally, as a teen you will first be concerned with your personal issues and problems. This is as it should be for the beginner. As the saying goes, you must learn to walk before you can run.

As you work with your Tarot cards, you will gradually access deeper levels. At the collective level, tarot symbols can be applied to the dynamics of the community or to the society at large. Read at the universal level, the symbols serve to decipher and explain the patterns found in nature. This deep level of interpretation connects us with the Divine Mind and its mysterious workings.

Into each life some change must fall. Often teens experience change as crisis, whether it is minor or major. One of the problems with being an adolescent is that events and inner states of mind and feeling are often exaggerated. The Fool is a good card to study in such times. One of my favorite astrologers, who has done much work on cycles, is the Swiss Alexander Ruperti. In *Cycles of Becoming*, he describes the crisis as follows:

Cycles are measurements of change. In order for any purpose to be realized, change must take place, and change necessarily involves crisis. Many have difficulty with the word *crisis*, confusing it with "catastrophe." [However,] it derives from the Greek word *krino*, "to decide," and means simply "a time for decision." A crisis is a turning point—that which precedes CHANGE.

Trump 0

THE FOOL

The Fool in a reading is an indication of change, and whether it is a major or a minor change, it requires trust. Many of us can feel change as threatening or upsetting. We all become attached to things as they are—the status quo—and anything that disturbs this can make us uncomfortable. When the Fool appears, he tells that change is necessary and the best way of handling it is to look upward and let go of fear.

Although this is not an easy task for anyone, it is especially difficult for a teen. So if change is a problem for you, study the Fool and use his carefree attitude as a model. Expect the best. Chances are you will make the adjustment without too much difficulty. You may be changing schools, going from junior high to high school, or entering college. You may be moving to another town, or your parents may be divorcing. Whatever is happening in your life when the Fool presents himself, take his appearance as a ray of hope. You are about to begin a new phase of your life.

Keys to Interpreting the Fool

A new beginning. The need to trust your own inner processes. Having faith that things will work out. Readiness to expand your awareness or begin a spiritual path. Naïveté and innocence. A leap into the unknown. A carefree attitude. Willingness to take a risk. Unexpected circumstances. New direction. Confidence. Optimism. Leaving the past behind. Nonconformity. New potential and possibilities opening up.

Historically, the Fool is related to the concept of the "holy fool," or the idea that madness or irresponsibility is divine. In the courts of medieval Europe, the king's fool (or the queen's) was given a special privilege to make fun of everything and everybody, for the amusement of the royal personages and their attendants. The word *silly* actually means "to be blessed," and in ancient times there were sacred revels when everyone behaved like a clown.

Trump I
THE MAGICIAN

THE MAGICIAN.

A powerful figure, the Magician represents worldly wisdom and the control of unseen forces that operate in human lives. The Magician's costume varies with different decks, but he always wears a belt, a symbol of wholeness. The Magician is a deeply complex symbol, seen displaying the tools of his trade—in most decks, these are the symbols of the Minor Arcana suits, each of which applies to an element: a pentacle for Earth; a sword for Air; a cup for Water; and a wand for Fire. Knowledge of these "elementals" is necessary to gain power in the world.

When the Magician appears in a reading, he signifies latent powers yet to be developed. He declares that you must learn to use your native talents correctly, both on the material plane and from a spiritual point of view. Mere worldly success, whatever that means to you—good grades, popularity, winning at sports, looking good, having lots of friends—is eventually empty unless it is based on correct spiritual principals. You must learn to use your intellect, intuitive ability, personal talents, and practical skills to mediate between the two worlds, both of which affect us all simultaneously. The Magician is a card of power, telling us that our nature is one with the nature of the universe. It brings the message that we have the ability to control things and events in our lives—as long as we go about it in the right way and for the right ends.

The Magician corresponds to Mercury, and to the Greek Hermes, messenger of the gods. He has the ability to communicate between the celestial and earthly realms. The Magician indicates that higher intuitive forces may appear as a flash of insight. He tells you to pay attention to your intuition.

Keys to Interpreting the Magician

You have goals and are trying to reach them. You need discipline. Your creative forces are being called into action. Decision making. Learning new skills. Inventive ability. Using your knowledge wisely. Special training. Technical mastery. Focused attention. A need to observe everything closely. Experimentation. New projects. Modern technological expertise.

Mythologically, the High Priestess is related to the Egyptian goddess Isis, queen of the intellect, who understands fully the workings of the Universe and is familiar with both the upper world and the underworld, where her husband Osiris reigns. She represents divine wisdom and deep understanding of the laws that underlie and unite both realms.

Trump II
THE HIGH PRIESTESS

The High Priestess represents the mystery that is life. Her appearance is an indication of something that has yet to be revealed. She symbolizes the feminine spiritual power of the Goddess from whom all life comes and to whom all returns in the ever spinning cycle that is life. Usually she sits or stands between two pillars that represent the opposites in this world of duality: good and evil, light and dark, truth and deception, positive and negative.

When the High Priestess appears, she hints that something within you is preparing to come forth. You need to pay more attention to your inner world of dreams, imagination, and intuition. An awareness of totality includes the night as well as the daytime personality and activities. Often, you are ready to accept the importance of developing this part of your life, but have been holding back out of fear or inertia. Another possibility is that you are hiding something that you need to face.

Keys to Interpreting the High Priestess

Your internal world needs attention. Spiritual forces are at work. Interest in platonic love. Time to look within for answers to your problems. Expect dream messages. Hidden influences. Study of the occult. Awareness of the invisible world. That which is beneath the surface. The need to reflect, meditate, pray. The need for counseling or advice from a wise person. Book learning and higher education. Developing talents.

THE EMPRESS

THE EMPRESS.

The Empress represents beauty and nurturance and the *social* concept of the maternal role in all its aspects of positive love and caring. When the Empress appears in a teen's reading, there is usually an issue around marriage or motherhood. Depending on your age, you may just be thinking about what marriage means and how you feel about it; or you may be looking forward to marriage or actively seeking it. You may even be pregnant, or know someone who is pregnant. The Empress may point to issues about your emotional and physical resources. Or maybe you are in a situation that requires deep, unconditional love and nurturing. This card relates to the caretaking process. You may have issues about your mother or some other significant mother figure, or to how you were mothered. Sometimes this card indicates an overbearing "smother mother." An excellent card to use for meditation upon issues of nurturance, of marriage commitment, or of abundance, the Empress is usually positive and can tell of pleasure in general.

Keys to Interpreting the Empress

Fruitfulness of any kind. Abundance, prosperity, material comfort. Creativity. Productive action. Personal growth. Nurturing yourself or others. Social standing as an issue. Physical love and affection on your mind. Preoccupation with sexual relations. Desire for more of all good things. Maternal instincts aroused. Moving from one stage of life to another. Relating to Mother Nature and Mother Earth.

The Empress is related to the planet Venus, which represents love and harmony. She is a powerful feminine figure, also linked to the ancient Mother Goddess. In the Christian tradition, she is akin to the Virgin Mary. As Venus symbolizes the Divine Feminine, the Empress is the primary sign of fertility—in Nature and in humans—and the need for *social responsibility*.

Trump IV

THE EMPEROR

The Emperor represents authority, the sort we associate with typical male power in the world. His attitude is one of passive kindness as the beneficent ruler of his empire. The Emperor is a positive symbol in terms of worldly power and wisdom, a teacher and a father figure, as the Empress is a mother figure. Yet he understands that to maintain peace and security, one must be willing and able to defend it. As the saying goes, "The price of freedom is eternal vigilance." He teaches the meaning and use of power in this world, telling that it is necessary sometimes to take up arms against negative or evil forces.

When the Emperor appears, look for issues related to authority. The issues may be in the teen's personal relationship with a father or with authority figures in general. The Emperor often surfaces when you are struggling to achieve independence, to become your own person, to come to terms with what "father" means in your life. Separation from parents is a crucial stage in human development and must be accomplished.

Mythologically, the Emperor is related to the father gods of the old religions: Zeus in the Greek pantheon, Jupiter in the Roman pantheon. The Scandinavians called him Thor, for whom Thursday is named. All were known for throwing thunderbolts or lightning. From a pagan perspective, because the Emperor *follows* the Empress, he represents her male companion, Pan being the most common figure. As consort to the Empress, he represents parenthood and masculine creativity.

Keys to Interpreting the Emperor

Being a grownup. Taking responsibility. Becoming your own authority. Self-assertion. Thinking rationally instead of emotionally. A desire to make your life meaningful in the world. Achievement of all kinds. Ambition. Security needs. Structure. Self-control. Making money. Taking on projects that matter. Dealing with authority figures. Finding a mentor or older adviser. Issues of paternity. Becoming employed. Politics. Respect.

Trump V
THE HIEROPHANT
(OR HIGH PRIEST)

THE HIEROPHANT

The Hierophant is also a figure of power and authority, but his is religious authority. Some decks entitle him "the Pope." He claims the power to decide what you must do and how you must live in order to achieve "salvation." The Hierophant denotes the education that forms a bridge between the physical world and the spiritual, like the knowledge of a priest whom some consider to be the intermediary between god and humans. He can be seen as a teacher to those who seek knowledge of the sacred Mysteries. When the Hierophant appears in a teen's reading, it is a clue that you are seeking a life philosophy to guide you, whatever your concept of god may be. There is also the possibility that you are disentangling yourself from an old belief system.

The Hierophant symbolizes *any* organized institution that exerts authority over its followers. Therefore, when the Hierophant appears, the idea of *choice* is paramount. At this stage of your spiritual development, you are challenged to remain a follower or to break away and find your own spiritual truth.

Keys to Interpreting the Hierophant

The Establishment. Professional counseling or advice. Higher moral authority. Appreciation of tradition. Conservative beliefs. External authority an issue. Institutions such as school and church. A search for meaning. Moral choice and development. Help from older, wiser men. Seriousness about your life. Conformity. Codes of conduct. Dealing with "the system." School officials. Role models. Traditional values. Doctors, teachers, advisors.

Mythologically, the Hierophant represents the quest for meaning in life. Connected to the sign of Sagittarius, which represents higher learning and the dissemination of knowledge, he guides the spiritual seeker to find a bridge between the inner and outer, the material and nonmaterial. He teaches that true wisdom and genuine spirituality go beyond the dogmas of organized religion and are based on the truth of the inner world of the psyche.

Mythologically, the Lovers reflect the great Greek goddess of love and beauty, Aphrodite, and the god Eros, her son. In the Roman pantheon, his name was Cupid, and his job was to shoot the arrows of love, considered a form of madness, at unsuspecting youths.

Trump VI
THE LOVERS

It is tempting to interpret this card as about romantic love, but what it is really about is the union of opposites. The appearance of the Lovers means that you have to make a choice about something significant in your life. True, this may refer to the choice of a love partner, but it could equally well refer to another important matter, such as which college to attend, or, in the case of a divorce of your parents, which parent to live with. The Lovers speak to the need for *discrimination* in the making of choices. The male and female figures usually shown on the card are symbols not only of human love and marriage but also of humanity's dual nature, full of opposite traits that need to be reconciled or lived with. The Lovers mark a crossroads. Be aware of all of the ramifications of the situation and choose carefully; consider your own development and also the needs of others involved.

Often in a teen's reading, the Lovers betoken issues around sexuality, usually the choice of whether to become sexually active or sexually involved with a different person. These are serious and eventful choices, not to be made lightly.

Keys to Interpreting the Lovers

Romance is in the air. Sexuality is blossoming. Temptation. A major life choice. A testing period. A choice between two options. Facing duality. Focus on love. Obstacles to love. Wanting a partner. Fantasizing about marriage. Conflict within. A fork in the road. Questions about commitment. A significant other. A new love interest. Reconciling opposites within or without. A need for decision. Partnership. Choosing a new path.

Trump VII
THE CHARIOT

The Chariot is a symbolic picture of the requirement to master and reconcile competing forces, both inner and outer. Its appearance announces your need to work toward something like the celebrated but seldom achieved "bipartisanship" of government. You are being advised to harness conflicting elements in your life. To do this, you need self-mastery, and a strategy determined by clear thinking and a sense of purpose. The Chariot in a reading is generally favorable, assuring you that you have the means to triumph over obstacles and stay the course you have set for yourself. Assistance may be coming as a result of your own strength and determination. Possibly you are in the middle of transforming your ways to create a firm foundation for your life and future aims. About movement, this card may indicate that you need to get moving and deal with reality. At a literal level, the Chariot refers to travel and transportation and could mean you're changing your mode of transport, maybe getting a car or a bike—some kind of wheeled vehicle.

Keys to Interpreting the Chariot

Control of yourself and your circumstances. Clarity of purpose. Determination. Steering a middle course. Resolving conflict, both inner and outer. Self-determination and assertiveness. Being centered and single-minded. Goal setting. Ambition. Making progress by staying on course. Strength of will and purpose. Charging ahead in spite of obstacles. Triumph over struggle and conflict. A new car. Wheels.

Mythologically, the Chariot is related to Helios, the Greek sun god who drove a chariot of fire across the heavens, and Sol, whom the Romans paraded in triumph after victory in war. The charioteer points to success and a focus on getting your energies harnessed. With this energy you can build a momentum that will carry you to triumph over all conflicting forces to find your true path in life. Guided by intuition and clear purpose, you are in the driver's seat of your own life.

Trump VIII
STRENGTH

(*Note:* Some decks number Strength as eleven and Justice as eight. Arthur Waite fixed Strength as eight; most new decks use his system.)

Usually depicted as a woman with a lion, this card is symbolic of self-confidence and inner strength. When Strength appears, it shows that you are in harmony with your "animal" or instinctive nature. You are exhibiting moral courage and fortitude. Strength indicates that you have come through difficulties and learned to rely on yourself. Your position is strong; you have suffered trials and tribulations without being defeated by them. The feminine principle can reconcile the mental-rational with the intuitive-instinctive nature because it is always in close touch with nature. We do not conquer our animal natures by brute force—a "masculine" approach—but by the gentle means of feeling our way into rapport with the instinctive side of our nature.

Strength counsels an inner strength and reliance on intuition in the situation. With patience and forbearance, spiritual strength will prevail over physical strength. You are being told to have faith in yourself and your inner processes.

Keys to Interpreting Strength

Intuitive ability. Inner strength. Power without force. Self-discipline. Self-confidence. Faith in one's abilities. Protection. Courage. Good health. Recovery. Renewed vitality. Feminine empowerment. Fortitude under stress. Success in your endeavors. Physical or athletic ability. Enthusiasm. High energy. Taking pride in yourself and your accomplishments. Self-protection. Building skills. Ethics. Self-control.

Strength is related to the ancient pagan goddess known as the "Lady of the Beasts." Personified by the Greeks as Artemis, goddess of the hunt, Strength also relates to the great and powerful feline goddesses of ancient Egypt: the lion-headed Sekmet, and Bast, ruler of love, beauty, and fertility. Strength may appear in a reading to a teen who is concerned about physical attributes. She signals positive acceptance of all that is feminine, no matter what the pop culture pushes as attractive.

THE HERMIT

The Hermit is a guide figure who radiates the wisdom of the archetypal old man, the sage of myth and legend. Wise in the ways of all the worlds, visible and invisible, material and non-material, he travels alone, a seeker after truth. He holds aloft a lamp, lighting the Way. As a Seeker, he has no rank, needs no adornment, carries no baggage. His purpose is to reveal your true direction. He carries a wooden staff that symbolizes his connection to Nature and the realm of the instincts. He is linked to Father Time and the planet Saturn, which symbolizes the natural limitations of human life. When the Hermit appears, he tells that you may need more solitude, or that you have withdrawn from your usual everyday world, either gladly or because you feel rejected. You may be going through a "loner" phase in order to gain perspective on your life. The Hermit can herald a mentor in real life, or a spiritual guide standing by awaiting your call through silent reflection. You may be on a quest for knowledge and deep understanding of the forces affecting you.

Keys to Interpreting the Hermit

Withdrawal from worldly concerns. Contemplation and meditation. Loneliness or isolation. Quiet time for study or reading. Being alone. Seeking counsel or advice from an older person. Self-examination. Discovery of the inner self. Needing space. Getting it together by yourself. Searching for Truth. Pondering the Mystery of Life. Seriousness. Enlightenment. Trusting inner guidance. Spiritual advice.

The guide figure may represent a counselor of some sort—a therapist or clergyperson—but usually it refers to inner guidance or a guide from the other side.

The appearance of the Hermit emphasizes that the quest for knowledge, both worldly and spiritual, is valuable for you at this time. For many teens, this means devotion to study, or the seeking out of a personal spiritual path. Or both. The Hermit draws you into yourself and there you find the needed guidance. Because of the Hermit's relation to the past, and to life's limitations, you may be struggling to free yourself of these.

The Wheel of Fortune is a reminder of the mysterious cycles of life, death, and rebirth. Mythologically, it is linked to the three Fates. This suggests the working of forces we can't see and attests to an intelligent order in life. The idea is that, in some mysterious way, we all participate in creating our individual destinies and are involved in directing the course our lives will take.

Trump X
THE WHEEL OF FORTUNE

The Wheel of Fortune is a reference to ancient symbolism for the wholeness of the world as produced by the ever turning cycles of life, death, and rebirth. When the Wheel of Fortune appears, it means that you have put something in motion and you now must await the outcome, usually favorable. You may have applied for a job or college. You may have begun a new friendship or romance. Even a chance encounter could have got the wheel turning. Whatever caused the motion of destiny, you are entering a new phase. You may soon be required to make an important decision about your next move in life. It's possible that an unexpected development will literally change your life.

The Wheel of Fortune depicts the idea expressed in the Rubáyiát of Omar Kayyám, roughly translated as, "The moving finger, having writ, moves on, nor all your charm nor wit can cancel half a line of it." This card refers to the cycles of life. It can point out opportunities for your growth and development.

Keys to Interpreting the Wheel of Fortune

Good luck. Things working out well. A second chance. A new cycle beginning. Progress. What comes around goes around. Awareness of consequence of action. An unexpected break. Change. Powerful forces are in motion to benefit you. A new chapter in your personal book of life. A need to accept what life offers. Fast-moving events. New direction. Faith and belief in universal processes. Learning to be adaptable.

Trump XI
Justice

When the Justice card appears in a reading, it is a call to order. Take note: you must carefully weigh many factors in whatever situation you are seeking advice. The Justice card tells you to seek guidance from your inner self and to consult human advisors. It recommends caution, prudence, and deliberation in a calm state of mind before you take action. In other words, use good judgment. Justice will be done if you yourself behave in a rational manner. You are being called upon to find balance—between your own needs and those of others, or in the combination of study, social life, romantic involvement, aims and goals, and extracurricular activities. A third party may assist you to get the fair result you deserve. This card can represent a lawyer, a judge, witnesses, law enforcement officers, and the like. If you are dealing with a legal matter, you can expect a positive outcome if you are in the right. You may have to make big decisions and learn serious lessons.

Keys to Interpreting Justice

Anything legal. Balance and harmony. Getting your act together. Consideration of others' opinions. Advice and counsel. Staying open-minded. Integrity. Fairness. Impartiality. Protecting your good reputation. Dealing with authority, especially the law. Weighing the pros and cons. Trusting your intuition. New and better forms of education. Taking proper thoughtful action. Avoiding bad company. Compromise in a relationship to achieve long-term success. Fighting for justice.

The Justice card is linked to Egyptian mythology. In that ancient tradition, the goddess Maat—whose name means "truth" and "justice"—used a pair of scales to determine if a person's soul would be allowed to pass into the underworld ruled by the god Osiris. Maat is also associated with the Hindu idea of *karma* that means, "As you sow, so shall you reap." This is echoed in the Buddhist tradition of cause and effect and in the Christian concept of repentance as the route to redemption.

THE HANGED MAN.

When the Hanged Man shows up, I ask my client, "Who's in charge of your mind?" Reflection may bring the surprise discovery that you aren't as much in charge of your mind as you believe. Lots of teens base their thinking on the opinions of their peers, parents, teachers, or friends. To be in charge of your mind you need to learn to *see* in new ways. It is the development of this capacity that the Hanged Man represents. Being in charge of your mind permits you to "create your own reality."

Trump XII

THE HANGED MAN

The Hanged Man is shown upside down, with one leg crossed behind the other knee; his arms are bent and his hands are behind his back. But his expression is serene. The suggestion is that he is seeking enlightenment, which he is to achieve by giving up superficial pleasures and trivial pursuits.

When he appears, he signals that you are spiritually ready for a major transformation. You are at a crossroads. You may have experienced an illness or a loss that shook up your way of life and made you aware that you need to make some changes. You now know there is more to life than money and material goods; you now seek a more spiritually oriented way to live your life. The Hanged Man's presence marks your readiness to commit to your inner growth. You may be feeling a need to get off by yourself, to take a break from ordinary life and reevaluate your priorities, to decide just what is and what is not important. You may be having a lot of difficulty letting go of an old pattern—a relationship, a group of friends, a belief system, over-dependence on your parents—or you may just be in a rut.

Keys to Interpreting the Hanged Man

A new perspective. A time for change. A need to set priorities. Where are you going with your life? Marching to your own drummer. Looking at the world differently. Sacrifice. Commitment. Being different from the crowd. Voluntarily letting go of stuff. Suspension of normal activities. Getting a fresh perspective. A transition period. Spiritual development. "Let go and let God." Finding your true Self. Contemplation. Rest. Relaxation.

The Death card tends to frighten people, but its grim depiction merely symbolizes the transforming powers—*not* actual physical death. It means the end of a cycle. Especially for teens, Death indicates the end of one phase of life and the beginning of a new phase. You might be leaving junior high for senior high, or high school for college. And you may feel this is a painful transition. However, it's all part of growing up, and growing up has never been easy. When a stage in your life ends, it's only natural to feel sad, even mournful. But as you grow up, you find new satisfactions in new situations, even if you have difficulties adjusting. Accept that something is over, and don't try to avoid the inevitable. You are in a process of transformation, and that's what life is all about. Always something must "die" so that what's new can come into being. It's *acceptance* of the change that lets you grow further. If you are depressed and Death appears, don't be upset. However, if you are having too many thoughts or fears about dying, discuss these with a responsible, trusted adult promptly.

Keys to Interpreting Death

Major life change. Transformation from one stage to another. Liberation from old, outworn patterns. The end of a cycle and the beginning of a new one. Change of status. Loss causing new ways of thinking. Discarding what isn't needed anymore. The end of a relationship or friendship. Leaving home. The end of childhood. Letting go of what's not working. A new lifestyle. Relocation. Loss of virginity. Divorce in family.

Death's number is thirteen, the number of witches in a coven. In the lunar calendar, the thirteenth month is the time of mystical regeneration and rebirth. Mythologically, Death is linked to the Hindu goddess Kali, who wears a necklace of skulls; and to the Greek god Hades, ruler of the underworld, called Pluto by the Romans. These are powerful figures. Teens are often preoccupied with ideas of death. They can be used as images for meditation and for learning that death is just another of life's phases.

TEMPERANCE.

Any vessel is symbolic of the great Mother Goddesses of antiquity. The human body is called the vessel of the soul. The pouring of the liquid between the two vessels in a continuous stream represents the constant intermixing of the material and spiritual planes and symbolizes the eternal flow of the mystical waters of life. Thus, both the figure—often an angel—and the cups are references to the feminine spirit of cooperation, balance, harmony, receptivity, and creativity.

Trump XIV

TEMPERANCE

The lovely Temperance card shows a figure pouring the elixir of life from a golden vessel into a silver one. As its name suggests, Temperance is about moderation and balance. Derived from the Latin *temperare,* which means to moderate, blend, or mix together harmoniously, Temperance appears when *patience* is needed. You are not in a position to make things happen. There's nothing to do but wait while the life energies are being combined. Learning to wait gracefully and constructively is an art well worth mastering. Doing nothing, *mindfully,* makes for spiritual progress. Knowing there will always be times when nothing *can* be done, it's vital to realize also that nothing *needs* to be done. Therein lies the state of grace. This is one of the great lessons of the Zen masters.

Temperance signifies that you are in a position to exercise your creative talents and to solve sticky problems through a temperate attitude without trying to rush things to a conclusion before they are ready. There may well be angelic influences at play in the situation. Be aware of invisible helpers.

Keys to Interpreting Temperance

Patience. Prudence. Taking the middle road. Proper timing. Being discreet. A balanced view of the situation. Looking at all sides fairly. Avoiding extremes. Creativity and new ideas. Different types of relationships. Reevaluation of attitudes. Sensitivity to others. Issues of caution, especially in sexual involvement. Healing of past hurts. Mercy and compassion. Forgiveness. Compromise. Tolerance. Moderation.

Trump XV
THE DEVIL

The Devil is another scary card, often shown complete with horns, hooves, a hairy tail, and a pitchfork. Human figures, one male and one female, are chained up, but the looseness of the chains implies self-imposed limitations. When the Devil appears, you need to reevaluate your relationship to material things, review relationships, especially abusive or harmful ones, and confront your attitudes toward society and the things of this world: in other words, you need to do a reality check. It's time to let go of whatever is holding you back—fears, hang-ups, inhibitions. Instead of using others to satisfy your needs, you are challenged to take responsibility for yourself in a positive manner. There may be a sexual factor in the situation that is messing up your life; you may know this but are resisting taking the right action to release yourself. Or maybe you are bound in some other kind of relationship from which you must separate for your own good. Whatever the situation, you are the only one who can change it.

Keys to Interpreting the Devil

Negative thinking. Caught in an untenable relationship. Taking charge of your own life. Overcoming guilt. Bad attachments. Confronting fears. Overdependency. Sexual problems. Depression and bad feelings about yourself. Self-imposed limitations. Conflict between material goods and spirituality. Power hunger. Manipulation of others. Finding it hard to let go of what is hurting you. Feeling trapped or stuck in the situation.

Mythologically, the Devil is connected to Great Pan, the ancient god who ruled all natural processes, including lust and sex. The Greeks named him Dionysos, the wine god known for drunkenness and sporting with satyrs. He is the horned god of pagan times, in whose honor female followers of the goddess religion held wild fertility rites. Christianity banned all pagan rituals, especially those including sexual activity, for the Church feared the power of these uninhibited annual rituals that included a sexual free-for-all.

The deep meaning of the Tower is *psychological*—and spiritual. Although its appearance represents ruin and devastation, and it predicts dramatic change, something is being destroyed so that something better can be put in its place. Even if the situation is sudden and shocking, you must accept that major change will ultimately benefit you. Hanging on to old patterns of behavior, thinking, or believing is holding you back. After you recover from being upset, you will find you have been liberated!

Trump XVI
THE TOWER

The Tower depicts a fortresslike construction being struck by lightning, in flames, or falling down. Like Death and the Devil, the Tower tends to strike fear when it shows up. But it is merely a warning that you must make changes or suffer the consequences. If you refuse to acknowledge a pressing need to make changes, you invite the universe to force them on you. Then, BAM! Along comes some seeming disaster—you get expelled from school, lose your romantic love, wreck your car, get seriously grounded—and you are finally into reality-check mode. The warning of the Tower is this: instead of stubbornly looking everywhere but where the problem lies, you must face facts and make changes promptly or you will pay the price. Old structures will be shattered by external influences so that you can grow into your real Self. After things come tumbling down, you will have the opportunity to rebuild, choosing to keep what is valuable and discarding what you don't need now.

Keys to Interpreting the Tower

Sudden change. A new way of life following upset. Disruption of your normal pattern. An amazing insight or revelation. Major upheaval leads to transformation. Recognition of structural flaws. Disillusionment. Release from old ways. New values. Confronting important issues. Collapse of well-made plans. Shucking off conventional ways of thinking. Disappointment leading to knowledge. Discarding what doesn't work.

Trump XVII
THE STAR

This lovely card often shows a naked female figure with stars in the bright background. The Star is always positive and suggests that you are receiving benefits. It betokens helpful people, creative inspiration, and a promise that you will get what you want (if it's good for you!). When the Star appears, you are encouraged to develop your abilities with self-confidence. Your desires are in sync with your correct life path. Following the Tower, it can reveal a recovery from some trauma or bad situation. You are coming into a new and happier phase of life. The Star is a reminder of all the magnificence of the Universe. Now is the time for you to ponder your potentials for growth. A gate to new directions and new successes has opened for you. You have achieved the right relationship between the material world and the spiritual realm and will be assisted in your efforts to grow. This celestial card corresponds to matters of your "soul life." It is a good time for using affirmations.

Keys to Interpreting the Star

Inspiration, intuition, inner wisdom, celestial guidance, protection, good fortune. Creative inspiration, spiritual growth, help from unseen forces. A guardian angel. Optimism and self-confidence. Enjoyment and pleasure. Faith and trust in your future prospects. Developing your special talent. Educational opportunity. Improved health. The end of a period of distress. Good news. Hope renewed. Happiness. Luck. Release.

The Sumerians were astronomical observers, whose tracking of the movements of the stars (planets) resulted in astrology. This celestial card has a strong connection to astrology, so this is a good time to have your horoscope read or to begin studying astrology. It is a time of fulfillment. When the Star appears, go outside and make a wish upon the first star you see. Your wish may come true. And when it does, be sure to give something back to show your appreciation and gratitude.

The Major Arcana and Their Meanings   59

THE MOON.

Symbolically, the Moon calls you to illuminate the unconscious side of your life, for in her subtle light you are able to see more of what is harder to perceive. The moon shines her soft light into the inner world, where Spirit dwells. In moonlight we can understand our spiritual yearnings and promptings more clearly than with the rational, daytime mind. We are more aware of the nuances of our feelings and inner perceptions.

Trump XVIII

THE MOON

The Moon is a magical, mysterious card emblematic of the things of the invisible realm—dreams, imagination, and psychic impressions. Its rich symbolism suggests you should pay more attention to your inner Self.

Traditionally the Moon refers to negative conditions such as deceit and self-deception, but these usually result from ignoring the inner world. The Moon notifies you to tie up loose ends associated with the past, especially with your mother or other females. If the Moon is related to negative cards in the spread, you are over-nurturing others while neglecting your own emotional needs. Conversely, if adjacent cards point to outward activities, you may be emerging from a long period of inner concentration, ready now to present your unique, creative self to the world.

Being a feminine symbol, the Moon's realm is what we *feel* and how we *respond*. It reflects all that is receptive in human nature. Your lunar self flows with the universal rhythms. The Moon affects everything and everyone on earth.

Keys to Interpreting the Moon

The feminine principle. Deep inner forces at work. Past conditions affecting the present. Mystery and romance. Poetry, music, creativity. A time to be receptive, to "tune in" to inner guidance. Escapism, fantasy. Changeability. Excess emotionalism. Negative moods. Uncertainty. Hunches. Awareness of things hidden or kept secret. Nature, animals, wild things. Visions. Counseling or therapy. Bringing up the past for examination.

Trump XIX
THE SUN

Like a beautiful sunny day that inspires good feelings, the Sun card calls up ease and pleasure. When it appears, it is an assurance that good things are coming into your life. Even if there are negative cards in the spread, the Sun lightens their influences considerably. The Sun is a happy card and is always indicative of beneficial things. Important efforts—such as preparing for and taking examinations—will succeed. The Sun relates to children and childhood and may indicate a birth. Attention is coming your way, possibly gifts. You are in a good mood, and luck is with you. Your everyday situations are improving. Life's a day at the beach. You can let go of previous worries and count on the sun shining on your enterprises; it's the dawning of a new day. Love and affection come easily. You are inspired to optimism and creativity. Being yourself isn't hard now, for you feel confident and secure in your own identity. You are developing your individuality. Feel free to express yourself and to set goals.

Keys to Interpreting the Sun

Success, optimism, achievement, general good fortune, prosperity, enthusiasm, honors, public recognition, happiness. Health, increased vitality. Ambition and confidence. Goal setting. Opportunity and advancement. Public recognition. Academic achievement and honors. A vacation in the sun. Celebration. Good relations with children. Fun and games. Aliveness. Exuberance. Playfulness. Satisfaction. Self-expression.

Mythologically and historically, the Sun, which represents the masculine principle, came to be worshipped as a god in many cultures. Its brilliant disk was seen to be the Giver of Life (as indeed it is). Hindus relate the Sun to their god Brahma. The Persians' sun god was Mithra; the Chaldeans was Bel; the Phoenicians, Adondi. The ancient Aztecs worshipped Quetzalcoatl. Each of these religious traditions believed the Sun represented the creative force of the Universe.

Of all the allegorical symbolism in the Major Arcana cards, Judgment is the most purely Christian image, suggesting the dreaded Day of Judgment when all souls will be judged and assigned to Heaven or Hell. However, other cultures have expressed the same idea, which is basically about a spiritual awakening. Today when events cause us to reevaluate our way of life, we refer to a "wake-up call." Mythologically, Judgment relates to the classical Greek Hermes, the guide of souls, and the magical powers of the inner world.

Trumps XX
JUDGMENT

Judgment heralds the awakening of a new or higher state of consciousness. You may be examining your beliefs or turning away from traditional or family ways to develop your own personal philosophy of life. Judgment represents an ending of a previous way of life, and a renewal. You are seeking new direction, making adjustments—through self-improvement and spiritual realizations—to become more fully who you are. This is a time for decision-making and change. For adolescents, this may include biological changes as well as changes in status. You may be going from high school to college, choosing a course of study or a career path. You may feel "dead" in your old situation, and you are ready to make life-altering changes. Judgment signals a unique opportunity to recast how you want to live. You are leaving an old way of life, ending a cycle, moving on to something bigger and better. People may be judging you—say, on a job or college application—but it is likely to be a favorable judgment. Newly free of doubt and indecision, you are experiencing a new freedom to be yourself.

Keys to Interpreting Judgment

A milestone. New, positive development. Endings and beginnings. Making judgments about right and wrong. Being judged, usually positively. Major change. Evaluating and being evaluated. A rite of passage, such as graduation. New opportunities. Letting go of old negative habits. Seeing the light. Taking stock. Passing examinations. Getting the rewards of past efforts. A clean slate. A legal decision in your favor. Healing.

Trump XXI
The World

The last numbered card of the Major Arcana, the World symbolizes the end of the Fool's spiritual journey. It usually shows a woman surrounded by an oval-shaped wreath made of vines, leaves, and flowers, representing the interconnecting spheres of life. When the World appears, you have successfully concluded a phase of your spiritual journey. Now you will receive what you have earned. Whole and complete, refreshed, you are ready to begin anew at a higher level. Blessings are yours for the asking—a rewarding career, entrance to the college of your choice, acceptance on a sports team, a feeling of alignment with your environment and the world at large. *Completion* is indicated—of goals, projects, studies. You have reached a stage of fulfillment and are in a position to develop your abilities to the max. The World refers to all spheres of life, so it indicates you are getting it all together, perhaps after a struggle. The whole is always greater than the parts. You are on the right path to your destiny.

Keys to Interpreting the World

The end of a long journey. New spiritual insights. Successful completion of something. A new cycle beginning. Living well in tune with the Universe. Harmony of mind, body, and spirit. Rewards, success, happiness. Connection to the wider world. Moving on. Approval. Freedom. Peace. Expanding your horizons. Travel. Commencement. Getting your just desserts. Fresh experiences. Winning. Achieving. Reaching your goals.

When you embark upon your personal spiritual journey, you invoke many unseen forces. These often manifest as guides that bring grace and show the way. Guides belong to the invisible world and, like angels, come in human or animal form. Interface with this world can cause you to be affected in a way that is life changing. With guides, you enter a world of invisible order that supports and nourishes your world and your life here.

More about the Trumps

THE TAROT JOURNEY

As you work with the Major Arcana cards, you will become aware that they represent a journey into the Self. This is a vast, almost unfathomable realm in which you can explore possible future events, gain experience from your past, and develop the ability to find amazing insights into your thoughts, actions, motivations, and behavior. You will come to better understand your moods and confusing or difficult states of mind. Your impulses, cravings, "irrational" ideas, and murky feelings will gradually become familiar to you.

It's always important to remember that although the Tarot can give you much information, it is only a *tool*. You are the master of your own destiny. As such, you are in control of how you choose to interpret the cards. As you have already seen, there are many possible interpretations, depending on the situation or question being asked, the position of any given card in the spread, and the other cards you draw for a layout. The position of the cards is a major factor in interpreting a spread. The purpose of studying each card individually—especially the Major Arcana—is to fix its various possible meanings in your mind so that when you see the card you will automatically recall these meanings and be able to choose the appropriate one for the moment.

Unfortunately, the Tarot has been used for fortune-telling, which means predicting the future. That is not its purpose, and it is best not to use it that way. Predicting the future is impossible—there are just too many variables to know anything for sure. Thus, the Tarot never predicts a single, inevitable outcome; instead, it gives pointers and leaves you (or the person you're reading for) the choice of what to do with the information. It's like a weather forecast that helps you to decide whether to stay home or go out, and also how to prepare if you are going to be out in bad weather—or good weather. To depend on a reading for making major life decisions is a mistake. It denies the concept of free will. No matter what the cards may say, you will *always* have a choice in the matter. It's thrilling to realize that the future isn't already decided—it's up to you to make the most of the possibilities available.

What the Tarot can do is to illuminate the nature of the present circumstances. When the reading indicates that you are on a path that is leading you where you want to go, then stay with that. If the reading indicates a path that leads to trouble ahead, you can adjust your behavior and attitude to avoid it. If the reading indicates that a bad situation is in progress, the Tarot may well point out ways to get out of it or to make it better. This is where your study of the card meanings comes in. By keeping your Tarot notebook, you can monitor your progress regularly.

In addition to the use of the Tarot for advice and counsel about a situation, there is quite another benefit that results from

"It is clear that civilization cannot evolve further until the occult is taken for granted on the same level as atomic energy."

Colin Wilson,
The Occult

your growing knowledge. As you broaden your studies and become adept at seeing the whole picture of a spread, you will have begun a process of activating your intuition to a high level. This is a major accomplishment. Scientists tell us that the majority of the time, most of us use only about 10 percent of our mental capacities (including both the rational left brain and the intuitive right brain), and that's when we are clicking along in high gear! Learning the Tarot is a good way to increase the amount of brain power available to you.

As you proceed through this book, you will begin to activate your power to make your dreams come true. Meditation on the cards creates deep understanding of the symbolic level of life, which goes on within you all the time even if you aren't aware of it. For example, in your dreams you create symbols every night.

In addition, you can use the cards for visualization exercises. These help strengthen positive images in your mind and reduce the impact of negative images. To use any particular card for visualization, you just need remove the card from the pack and concentrate on it. Then, with your eyes closed, see in your inner mind the outcome you want to achieve. For example, if you are faced with a dilemma involving choosing between two love interests, you could use the Lovers for visualization. As you imagine yourself one of a pair of lovers, you release the powers of your unconscious mind to make the right choice between two people.

The more you use the Tarot, impressing its images and meanings upon your inner mind, the better able you will be to use the Tarot for your specific purposes. It can help you with all sorts of questions—such as "What's the likely outcome of my final exam?" or "What's the likely outcome of my application to _____ (fill in the blank)?" For high school and college students, frequent interactions with the Tarot can be an aid to learning your regular studies, because it activates learning centers in the brain you don't usually use. Many students who use

"Psychologists have hitherto failed to realize that imagination is a necessary ingredient of perception itself."

Immanuel Kant,
Critique of Pure Reason

the Tarot find they are inspired creatively to carry out both scientific and artistic projects. Some who hadn't previously considered themselves to be very scientific or artistic find out they have hidden talents. Using the Tarot regularly is an aid to the function of memory, and frequent use of your interpretive skills helps general learning. Keeping a Tarot notebook is good practice for your developing writing skills as well. In short, there are many benefits to studying the Tarot. It can open doors to possibilities you haven't yet imagined. As you begin and continue your Tarot journey, you will find guidance that may amaze you. You will discover new and wonderful places inside yourself that otherwise would have remained unknown. And always, the Tarot can help you to understand the meaning of your daily experiences with other people and with various situations that arise.

Significators

Many layouts call for the use of a significator. This is a card chosen to represent, or signify, you or another person, a group, a situation, or an event. The trick is to choose a card that seems like an apt symbol for the person or situation. Arthur Edward Waite recommended using a significator as "the most suitable for obtaining an answer to a definite question." Below are listed some keywords to help you when choosing which card to use as a significator.

O THE FOOL A child or young person. Innocence or lack of life experience. Adventure of any kind, such as travel or a trip. A decision involving risk.

I THE MAGICIAN Someone with latent talent. The potential for power of any kind. A person with artistic ability. Putting ideas to a practical use.

II THE HIGH PRIESTESS Secrets or someone who is keeping a secret. A quest for unusual or occult knowledge. A scholar or researcher. Psychic ability or a wise woman.

III THE EMPRESS A mature woman in a position of authority, wealth, and power. A female in politics. An Earth Mother personality. A pregnant woman or mother.

IV THE EMPEROR A man of authority, wealth, and power. A public figure. Male authority figure—your father, a coach, a cop, or a lawyer. Your boss, an older male relative.

V THE HIEROPHANT A teacher, professor, priest, minister, or mentor figure. A representative of an established institution. Someone in charge of awards or grants.

VI THE LOVERS Two people who have to cooperate with each other. A steady couple. A love relationship or a friendship. Any situation affecting two people.

VII THE CHARIOT A messenger or a message. Someone in transportation or the military. The need to control a situation. Getting a group organized.

VIII STRENGTH A strong woman or a forceful person. Someone with charisma and charm. Courage is required. An athletic competition. A situation requiring self-control.

IX THE HERMIT A seeker of knowledge. Need for guidance. An elderly person. A recluse. A wise man who instructs you. Being alone. Examining the past.

X WHEEL OF FORTUNE Does not represent persons. Used to represent situations already in process where the outcome is not yet known. Hoping for the best.

XI JUSTICE Someone who must make an important decision. A lawyer, a judge, an arbitrator. Anyone involved in a lawsuit who deserves a fair outcome.

XII THE HANGED MAN Someone at a crossroads or a standstill. A person who has retreated from ordinary life, and is seeking a new way or a new perspective on things.

XIII DEATH Death is not usually used as a significator but can represent a major transformation, such as the end of a relationship, or loss of any kind.

XIV TEMPERANCE A healer—a nurse, doctor, psychotherapist, or practitioner of alternative healing. Someone who needs healing. A protective figure.

XV THE DEVIL Someone who is depressed or suicidal. A person who feels trapped. Any restrictive situation limiting your progress.

XVI THE TOWER The Tower is not used to signify a person. It can represent a chaotic situation that is out of the person's control.

XVII THE STAR Someone with humanitarian tendencies. A helper figure. An entertainer. An artist. A beautiful person. Someone trustworthy. A spiritual person.

XVIII THE MOON Someone who is dreamy and preoccupied. A night person. A virgin. A mother figure. A wise woman who gives advice. An intuitive person or psychic.

XIX THE SUN Use for children or issues about children. Good when you want to illuminate a situation. A cheerful person. A beach lover. Virile man.

XX JUDGMENT Someone seeking the truth. A judge or judicial matter. A person in a new stage of development. Someone in transition. A pending judgment.

XXI THE WORLD Winners. Achievers. A fulfilled person. An environmentalist. World travelers. Someone who has reached a goal. A successful person.

Tarot Play Exercise

LEARNING TO USE SIGNIFICATORS

Think about the people in your life—parents, teachers, relatives, friends, lovers, and so forth—and pick out which trump you would choose as a significator for each one. Make a list. Then pick out significators for yourself, to apply to the different situations that concern you at present. Make a list.

Each day, choose one of the significators on your list and write down everything that comes to mind about the card and the person you have chosen it to represent, or the situation about which you are thinking. Do not refer to the interpretations but just write down what comes to you intuitively, just by studying the illustration on the card.

Later, compare your impressions with the descriptive interpretations given in this book, or with any standardized interpretations from other Tarot books. Be sure to focus on one card at a time.

Tarot Play Exercises

MORE MAJOR ARCANA ACTVITIES

Here are some other things you can do with the Major Arcana cards in order to get to know them better:

- Separate the cards of the Major Arcana into different piles according to whether you think they are positive or negative. Examine each card in each pile separately and decide why you think it belongs in that pile. Analyze your response by exploring the symbols and the colors. (If you have two decks, do this exercise with the other deck, too, since it will have different symbols and colors.) In your Tarot notebook, write out your reaction to each card and why you feel it to be positive or negative.

- Choose a card that especially appeals to you and write a short essay, a story, or a poem about the card. Fill in the name and number of the card at the top of the page in your notebook before writing about the card. Describe why you like the particular card.

- Use your imagination to create characters who might be real people from the cards of the Major Arcana. Throw a pretend party for as many as you like and imagine how they would react to each other. What would they like to do at a party? Who would you have the most fun with? What kind of guests would they make? What would you serve to eat and drink? How would your parents and friends react to these guests?

- Incubate a dream using one of the Major Arcana. Ask for specific answers to a question. Put the card under your pillow that night. Write down your dream in your Tarot notebook as soon as you wake up.

The Major Arcana and the Signs of the Zodiac

Because I find that there are amazing correspondences between the Tarot cards and astrology (and I'm a professional astrologer as well as a Tarot master), I am going to describe the astrological correspondences, which are a result of my years of experience using both methods. For the reader unfamiliar with astrology, I recommend my book *Teen Astrology* as a wonderful adjunct to this book. Naturally, you can use the Tarot with no knowledge of astrology, but knowledge of the planets and the signs of the zodiac as they relate to the Major Arcana will add to your understanding of the Tarot.

"The horoscope is a blueprint of our character. Character IS destiny. There is nothing static in the universe in which we dwell. We can change by changing our attitudes and patterns of behavior. In so doing we change our destiny. . . . The stars impel but do not compel."

Isabel Hickey,
Astrology, a Cosmic Science

AQUARIUS KEY CHARACTERISTICS

◈ Intuitive
◈ Innovator
◈ Awakener
◈ Humanitarian
◈ Undisciplined
◈ Iconoclast
◈ Liberator
◈ Revolutionary

MERCURY KEY CHARACTERISTICS

◈ Communications
◈ Thinking
◈ Messenger
◈ Ideas
◈ Adaptability
◈ Cleverness
◈ Superficiality
◈ Lack of focus

O The Fool

The Fool is related to the sign of *Aquarius,* which represents mental activity and the most advanced scientific thinking. Aquarius is concerned with humanity at large, and also with all the differences—and tolerance for those differences—between persons and groups of people. Aquarius is ruled by the planet Uranus, which has to do with the uniqueness of each person. It symbolizes abstract thinking and unusual courage and daring in quest of life's adventures—just as the Fool meets his encounters without fear. Aquarius represents nonconformists and humanitarians. The Aquarian spirit is forward-looking, even futuristic, and loves all kinds of new experiences, even dangerous ones. Old-fashioned, square thinking and activities bore Aquarius. This is an energy that is strongly individualistic, sometimes rebellious, always free-spirited, and eager to live life as an experiment.

I The Magician

The Magician is related to the planet *Mercury.* Curiously, Uranus, who is known as the cosmic magician and rules magic and invention, is the higher octave of Mercury, the planet of the mind and mental activities. Mercury is *exalted* in the sign of Aquarius, which means it functions at its highest level in Uranus. Thus, relating it to the Magician is more complex than astrologers generally credit. Mercury governs all communication—writing, speaking, learning, commerce—and all kinds of messages both spoken and written. He is all about the mind and mental activity. Mercury rules Gemini, an air sign, and the Magician is said to rule the element of air. Mercury also rules Virgo, an earth sign. This correlates to the Magician's ability to communicate between the realms of spiritual and earthly consciousness, a skill that often results in flashes of insight. When the Magician appears, check out your Mercury placement.

II The High Priestess

The High Priestess is related to the *Moon.* She wears the "horns of the Moon" on her headdress. The Moon is exalted in the sign of Taurus, the Bull, whose horns symbolize the Moon. The realm of the moon is our deepest inner self, our needs, memories, feelings, moods, and internal rhythms. The Moon rules the sign of Cancer, a water sign representing the instinctive nature, or what I call the "invisible world." The High Priestess is about secrets, or something yet to be revealed, and about the mystery that is Life. Cancer symbolizes emotional relatedness, memory, and the invisible side of life experienced only through our feelings.

The Moon has a hidden side that we never see. It helps us to illuminate what is occurring inside ourselves, to become more aware of feelings and inner perceptions, and to tune in to the spiritual vibrations of others.

MOON KEY CHARACTERISTICS
- Mothering
- Feeling-oriented
- Instinctive
- Nurturing
- Dependent
- Oversensitive
- Moody
- Needy

III The Empress

The Empress is related to the planet *Venus,* whose way is through relating—to others, to the desire nature, to the outside world. The planet of love, beauty, desire, and pleasure, Venus represents our affections and what we value in our social lives and in society in general. Venus symbolizes the deeply feminine part of all human beings, male as well as female, showing our capacity for loving and affectionate relationships with others, not just sexual ones. Venus is exalted in Pisces, the sign of higher spirituality that is ruled by Neptune, which works with transcendental vibrations to make romantic love an experience of singing in tune with the harmony of the spheres. As the "marriage card," the Empress suggests married love and children of a marriage as the ideal condition of true love.

VENUS KEY CHARACTERISTICS
- Attraction
- Desires
- Affections
- Sexual Love
- Sentiment
- Cravings
- Dependency
- Promiscuity

ARIES KEY CHARACTERISTICS

- Enthusiastic
- Active
- Adventurous
- Energetic
- Pushy
- Headstrong
- Foolhardy
- Impulsive

TAURUS KEY CHARACTERISTICS

- Affectionate
- Practical
- Determined
- Patient
- Possessive
- Materialistic
- Stubborn
- Unyielding

IV The Emperor

The Emperor is related to the sign of *Aries,* which symbolizes *action* such as leadership, initiative, and new ideas. As the first sign of the zodiac, Aries is about beginnings of all kinds. It is the energy of a leader, not a follower, the primal energy that gets things going. A self-starter, Aries is always on the lookout for adventure. This sign loves an exciting challenge, project, or experience. Under the dominion of the planet Mars, the principle of action in any and all spheres, this vibrant sign represents courage and forthrightness. The ruler of the traditional male attributes of which our society approves—sexual prowess, courage, energetic action, protectiveness, and valor—Aries applies to girls as well as boys, women as well as men, because both sexes have this energy though usually they express it differently.

V The Hierophant

The Hierophant is related to the sign of *Taurus*, the most earthy of the Earth Signs. Taurus symbolizes the realm of the physical senses and the material plane, which includes the accumulation of possessions and the maintenance of the status quo. Taurus's fixed nature gives patience. Though it may seem slow, it rests firmly on a base of certainty and self-confidence, secure in the knowledge that tomorrow is another day and that rushing about will not make the sun rise any sooner. Rooted in the physical world, Taurus exemplifies worldly concerns and institutions that endure over time—institutionalized religion, academia, the legal system. Taurus's natural instinct is to accumulate *and* to maintain both goods and institutions. The Hierophant therefore is a representative of what is permanent or enduring in the established social order.

VI The Lovers

The Lovers are related to the sign of *Gemini,* which epitomizes the dual nature of humanity (male and female, rational and intuitive). Symbolized by the Twins, this duality is clearly evident. Gemini's nature is to change, and change it does, sometimes with alarming rapidity, as anyone who has been in love can testify. But the Lovers card is not to be taken at face value. Rather than referring to a romantic situation, it is about the need to reconcile opposites, whether they concern two people in conflict or an inner conflict with oneself. Gemini is ruled by the planet Mercury. In her excellent book *The Mercury Method of Chart Comparison,* Lois Rodden comments that Mercury "opens the gates between two people, showing a clear picture of both the attitude and the circumstances between them."

GEMINI KEY CHARACTERISTICS
- Communicative
- Quick-witted
- Variety-seeking
- Spontaneous
- Superficial
- Scattered
- Distractible
- Nervous

VII The Chariot

The Chariot is related to the sign of *Cancer,* whose symbolic image is the Crab, a creature known for its ability to hold on. The Charioteer is seen holding firmly to his steeds. This represents the sheer tenacity of the life force. Cancer is ruled by the Moon, a connection to the Great Mother that affirms the power of the inner life-force. The stage of development corresponding to Cancer requires you to take charge of your own development, to learn mastery over your opposite tendencies, and to proceed no matter what obstacles stand in your way. Cancer's primary characteristic is to never let go—if a crab is grasping something with one claw, you have to cut off the claw to get the object loose. Cancer is an extremely powerful sign, representative of motherhood and family and the pulsating force of Life itself.

CANCER KEY CHARACTERISTICS
- Intuitive
- Nurturing
- Traditional
- Tenacious
- Illogical
- Dependent
- Living in the past
- Clinging

LEO KEY CHARACTERISTICS

- Dramatic
- Courageous
- Fun-loving
- Self-expressive
- Attention-seeking
- Self-glorifying
- Self-centered
- Insensitive

VIRGO KEY CHARACTERISTICS

- Orderly
- Intelligent
- Discriminating
- Logical
- Routinized
- Worrying
- Analytical
- Sequential

VIII Strength

Strength is related to the sign of *Leo,* a fire sign that symbolizes the heart center, from which all of your life energy flows and to which it returns. Ruled by the Sun, Leo depicts the creative individual who is bent on energizing potential into reality. Leo is the sign of the personal ego; Leo has extremely strong needs for self-expression and admiration. A natural leader, not easily discouraged, Leo follows through on everything with persistence and devotion. Leo betokens sustained energy, expressive action, and creativity. The Lion, representing the Eternal Flame, is an imperial symbol used on the royal coats of arms of many noble houses of Europe. Astrologically, the Sun stands for the individual and the essence of Spirit. Therefore, it signifies each person's individual connection to the divine Light Source and the archetypal father concept.

IX The Hermit

The Hermit is related to the sign of *Virgo,* which symbolizes the quest for perfection, often pursued in solitude. Virgo calls forth the Ideal Truth derived from contact with the divine essence, or Spiritual Guidance, and knowledge harvested from the fields of experience. Mental and serious, Virgo will work long and hard in the pursuit of knowledge and the performance of duty. Excellent critical faculties give Virgo high esthetic standards, but "art for art's sake" is of no interest. A practical sign, always looking to serve a purpose, Virgo wants to learn everything it can, with an emphasis on what is practical and useful. It aims toward being useful to others, especially in terms of passing on knowledge. Mercury, which rules both Virgo and Gemini, gathers information; Virgo sorts and analyzes the information so as to classify it and put it to practical use.

X Wheel of Fortune

The Wheel of Fortune is related to the planet *Jupiter* and the sign of Sagittarius. Jupiter represents ideological systems of thought, both philosophical and religious. Human social order is based on institutions. Jupiter serves as the interface between the individual and the institution. Jupiter manifests the Higher Mind— higher education and spirituality—and, consequently, goes beyond the purely rational to gain understanding of the universal principles on which thought is based. This desire for the grand overview is an example of Jupiter's integrative function, which is primarily social. Jupiter is exalted in Cancer, symbolic of the home, where learning is first encountered. As the family is the basic unit of society, Jupiter shows our development beyond the purely personal sphere outward to integrate with the larger society.

XI Justice

Justice is related to the sign of *Libra,* symbolized by a blindfolded woman holding a set of scales, the most common representative of impartial justice. An air sign, Libra is mental in nature, concerned with balance and harmony. It represents one-on-one relationships such as marriage and business partnerships. A complex Sign, Libra symbolizes the more abstract side of relationships, rather than the purely personal. In the Libran view, marriage is more of a social contract, not something you do simply for personal or romantic purposes. Libra, the seventh sign of the zodiac, desires whatever is balanced and harmonious, from marriage and esthetics to fairness in law. The Planet Saturn is exalted in Libra, and Saturn stands for what is stable, socially desirable, enduring, and without frivolity. Marriage!

JUPITER KEY CHARACTERISTICS
- Expansiveness
- Optimism
- Enthusiasm
- Abundance
- Ethics
- Principles
- Overexpansion
- Society

LIBRA KEY CHARACTERISTICS
- Relating
- Approval-seeking
- Diplomatic
- Indecisive
- Refined
- Impartial
- Artistic
- Conventional

NEPTUNE KEY CHARACTERISTICS

- Transcendental
- Mystical
- Escapist
- Creative
- Unrealistic
- Inspired
- Compassionate
- Addictive

SCORPIO KEY CHARACTERISTICS

- Mysterious
- Secretive
- Paranoid
- Intense
- Brooding
- Impenetrable
- Sexual
- Compulsive

XII The Hanged Man

The Hanged Man is related to the planet *Neptune,* inspirer of prophecy and visions, symbol of all that is mystical, other-worldly, and inspirational. At its highest, Neptune is the "celestial musician" who, unheard by the physical ear, is yet known to dreamers, artists, musicians, and poets. We can learn of our true purpose in the Universe through the energies of Neptune. Ruler of the sign of Pisces—the last and most mysterious sign of the zodiac—Neptune's vibration of cosmic consciousness simply flows out into the world. His is the realm of love that has risen beyond the personal to the universal. To express this kind of love often means self-sacrifice. Neptune is exalted in Cancer, a sign related to emotions (see the Chariot). But the Hanged Man summons the expression of emotions that are universal and forces that are transcendental.

XIII Death

The Death card is related to the sign of *Scorpio,* ruled by the planet Pluto, symbol of the transformative powers and of life's ultimate mysteries—sex and death, rebirth and regeneration. Astrologers associate the process that takes place in the underworld of the psyche with powerful Pluto, who sends messages about that dark and mysterious realm of our being by way of dreams and, sometimes, compulsive or destructive behaviors. Scorpio, the fixed water sign, is concerned with the processes of destruction and renewal, or transformation. Another word for transformation is *regeneration,* the process that breaks down the previous form and regenerates it into something new. For example, vegetation rots and becomes nutrients for new vegetation. At the time of conception, sperm and ovum both "die" when they become the embryo.

Births and Deaths

As we examine the dynamics of relationships closely, we notice a subtle grammar encoded in the way events unfold for others in relation to changes in our own life. This is especially evident in the great transitions of birth and death. In the news of children being born, ours or those of people around us, we may recognize powerful signposts of new beginnings taking place in our own lives. News of deaths often carries metaphors of significant closings or transformations in related areas of our experience.

For instance, astrologer Laurence Hillman has described the uncanny way the births of his two children coincided with business projects he had started. We often see the same phenomenon in the lives of prominent individuals, as when an actor's first child is born just when he has made a major new career move, or when an author announces the birth of a child just as she is offered a book contract from an important publisher. Amidst the flurry of biographical trivia to emerge during the trial of O.J. Simpson was the fact that his first child was born on the day he won the prestigious Heisman Trophy.

Deaths are similarly significant. Actor Richard Burton's death, to which his alcoholism and life of general excess contributed, occurred precisely as his longtime lover and ex-wife Elizabeth Taylor was emerging from life-transforming treatment for her alcoholism. In a symbolic sense, Burton had indeed "died" for her. The deaths of parents often seem to coincide closely with major changes or developments in their children's careers, as when George Bush's mother died near the time of his defeat by Bill Clinton; or when Russian leader Boris Yeltsin's mother died just as his authority was seriously challenged by a revolt by political opponents.

Ray Grasse, *The Waking Dream*

◈ Outgoing
◈ Expansive
◈ Optimistic
◈ Straightforward
◈ Ethical
◈ Freedom-loving
◈ Exploratory
◈ Outspoken

SATURN KEY CHARACTERISTICS

◈ Practical
◈ Disciplined
◈ Structured
◈ Restricted
◈ Limited
◈ Cautious
◈ Mature
◈ Restrained

XIV Temperance

Temperance is related to the sign of *Sagittarius,* the zodiac's seeker after Truth. Interested in all forms of knowledge—especially higher forms—Sagittarius represents Mind at its highest level of development. It is concerned with universal values and what is best in humanity. Learning is its forte. In addition, this spiritually oriented sign signifies those institutions that bind society together and teach ethics and morality. Thus, it has a connection with religion, but not necessarily established religion. The Sagittarian influence usually goes toward universality rather than a particular religious system. Expansive Jupiter rules. Jupiter, the Archer, is devoted to personal freedom—freedom of choice, of movement, of self-expression. As an advocate of intellectual freedom, this sign wants to know the absolute Truth underlying surface realities.

XV The Devil

The Devil is related to the planet *Saturn,* old Father Time himself. This Planet exemplifies the need for self-discipline and for the acceptance of the limitations of human life that are unavoidable. Saturn informs about structure and hard work. Ruler of the Sign of Capricorn, Saturn has lessons to teach and insists that you learn them, or the lessons are repeated until you "get it." However, once you've knuckled down and done your necessary homework, the old man grants 'goodies' in the form of worldly knowledge and the workings of practical reality. And certainly we all need to know about that! As a teen, you are in your first Saturn cycle, which lasts until you are about twenty-nine years old, and during those years you are always in the process of learning life's (sometimes hard) lessons. Learn them well! Make friends with Saturn.

XVI The Tower

The Tower is related to the planet *Mars*. This red planet is all about energy and how we use it. Energy can be tamed, like when you flick on the electric light switch, or it can be explosive—like the lightning bolts you see on most decks hitting the Tower and crashing it down. When you use your energies properly, you have them contained and under your control. But when use them improperly or bottle them up, you're asking for trouble, usually in the form of some kind of sudden destruction. Mars is also identified with sexuality, and as you may already know, sexuality can cause any number of explosive situations if it is not handled with utmost care. Teens often have trouble coping with their emerging sexual impulses and needs, and need to learn to use this powerful energy constructively and with all due caution. Energy needs to be regulated to be effective.

MARS KEY CHARACTERISTICS
- Drive
- Aggression
- Action
- Physicality
- Sexuality
- Anger
- Boldness
- Impetuous

XVII The Star

The Star is related to the sign of *Aquarius.* This sign sees everything in the spirit of universal love and friendship. It is about the idea of the individual as a part of a cooperative, larger whole—universality. The celestial illustrations on most Star cards hint that the entire Universe is being invoked. The idea here is that with the all-encompassing viewpoint you can freely cross all man-made boundaries at will and experience things new and different. It's the sign of the explorer, the advanced scientist, whatever is cutting edge. Ruled by Uranus, called the Higher Mind, this air sign is very mental and likes abstract thought. It can travel the airwaves of the cosmos without ever leaving home by its process of mental abstraction. Not good with personal emotions, Aquarius prefers the coolness of thought where the sky's the limit!

AQUARIUS KEY CHARACTERISTICS
- Humanitarian
- Innovative
- Friendly
- Unusual
- Emotionally cool
- Unorthodox
- Tolerant
- Individualistic

PISCES KEY CHARACTERISTICS

◈ Sensitive
◈ Imaginative
◈ Compassionate
◈ Escapist
◈ Creative
◈ Impressionistic
◈ Vulnerable
◈ Impractical

SUN KEY CHARACTERISTICS

◈ Individuality
◈ Father Spirit
◈ Consciousness
◈ Rational
◈ Will
◈ Drive
◈ Creativity
◈ Self-conscious

XVIII The Moon

The Moon is related to the sign of *Pisces,* which is all about the world of dreams, inspiration, and the desire to merge with the Cosmic Consciousness. Just as moonlight is actually reflected sunlight, Pisces is a reflection of the ephemeral nature of its ruler: Neptune, god of all that is invisible, hard to grasp, visionary, subtle, artistic, and psychic. The Pisces image of two fish swimming in opposite directions suggests the conscious mind on one side and the unconscious on the other, never quite getting together but forced to live side by side. Or you might say that one fish represents the physical body, which has to live here on earth and deal with its limitations, while the second fish represents the urge to blend into the universal Whole. Astrologically, the Moon personifies the Soul, the link between matter and spirit. Heed her gentle light's guidance!

XIX The Sun

The Sun is related to the sign of *Leo,* which it rules. A happy card, the Sun can be relied on to bring light into your life, just as the sun up above shines every day, even when it's raining. Called the Light of the Soul, the Sun astrologically represents your best self. This is what you are striving to achieve and what connects you to the Divine Source. As the center of our planetary system, the Sun is at the heart of the horoscope. It is about your potential for fulfillment of the qualities you were born with, a process of coming to consciousness that lasts a lifetime. It's the answer to why you are here on Earth, where you should go with your life, and what your ultimate purpose is. And you do have a purpose, or you wouldn't be here! The Sun is your innate vitality, source of your energy and ambition. It's also the symbol of the archetypal Father.

XX Judgment

The Judgment card is related to the planet *Pluto,* lord of the underworld in Greek and Roman mythology. Pluto is known as the "transformer," for whatever he touches undergoes a transformation—becomes something else. He is the bottom-line fundamental of life, for without transformation there is only death and no rebirth. A force to be reckoned with, this powerful energy is what allows for individual regeneration, which is ultimately what regenerates society, one person at a time. Exalted in Leo, the sign of self-awareness, Pluto energies often manifest as a "wake-up call," as shown by the trumpeter on the Judgment card. We all are given the task of regenerating ourselves in order to do the same for our society, but teens more than anyone bear this burden today. Bringing yourself up to full awareness must be your primary goal.

PLUTO KEY CHARACTERISTICS

- Transformer
- Regenerator
- Revitalizer
- Powerful
- Renewer
- Annihilator
- Redeemer
- Metamorphosis

XXI The World

The World is related to the sign of *Capricorn.* A social sign, Capricorn represents the world leader, or CEO type. Its animal symbol, the Goat, promises that Capricorn will continue to climb tirelessly and nimbly until it reaches the top of the mountain. But this is not purely for individual gain, for Capricorn represents the general social order and the authority that goes with it. It also implies doing things correctly, in an orderly and organized manner. It plays by the rules and expects others to do the same. Ruled by Saturn, the taskmaster of the zodiac, Capricorn works hard for success and then revels in its achievements. However, it is more interested in social values than personal freedom and will sacrifice the latter for the former—and insist that those under its command do the same! Representative of all authority figures, Capricorn is no doubt the most *worldly* Sign.

CAPRICORN KEY CHARACTERISTICS

- Serious
- Hard-working
- Traditional
- Trustworthy
- Practical
- Disciplined
- Dominating
- Rigid

Teen Astrology

Guess what? There's an entire astrology book written just for teens. In fact, I wrote it just for you because your teen years are the ideal time to learn to understand your own inner dynamics and go after the life you really want. Astrology is one of the best tools available for gaining insight into oneself and one's relationships with others.

Teen Astrology tells you about all your planets—and there are ten in your chart. It shows how the Sun represents your outer personality, that the Moon reflects the inner self, and how Venus, who rules matters of the heart, interacts with Mars, who governs sex and passion. There's more, too, including how to deal with your *parents*. Best of all, you don't need to know any astrology. Everything you need is in the book, including tables to look up your planets.

The title is *Teen Astrology: The Ultimate Guide to Making Your Life Your Own*, by M. J. Abadie. Teens from all over have written me to say how much they were helped by reading it. So check it out at your local bookstore or log onto amazon.com to get a copy of this special teen-friendly book.

Interpreting the Major Arcana in a Reading

Having come to the end of the Fool's journey, you have amassed a considerable knowledge of the archetypal symbols that form the backbone of the Tarot. Now that you have studied the basic meanings of the trump cards, you are ready to use them in actual readings. When interpreting them in a reading, it is important to be aware of the many layered meanings possible for each card. Not all apply to a particular question or situation. There are three levels on which you can interpret the Major Arcana: (1) practical, (2) intuitive, and (3) spiritual. It will be up to you and the nature of the question to determine which level is appropriate. By learning the various interpretations and practicing, you will be able to readily see which meanings apply to which categories or levels. (There are so many possibilities that no one book can exhaust all the meanings; it's best to study several books, over time.)

LOVE AND SEX

Sex is never far from a teenager's mind, no matter what adults might want to believe, and I'm a realist about the matter. We all yearn for love, and teens are intensely curious about sex. *But* there are pitfalls, especially if you are looking for love as a way out of a bad situation. Take my advice: *first learn to love yourself.* Then you will have a much better chance of success when you try to love another person.

If you suffer from a bad self image, send love to yourself. You can climb to the stars on a beam of self-love, which can be your secret weapon in times of trouble. Speak words of love to yourself daily. Affirm in thought, speech, and writing that you are a wonderful person worth your love. Treat yourself gently and with respect at all times.

Many teens will want to use the Tarot for divinatory, or predictive, uses. Young adults in particular are eager to get information about their future, or about how a current situation will unfold. When I began to write this book for teens, I decided to focus on the issues that are of most interest to your age group. Although I have given general basic interpretations in the previous chapters, I'll now become more specific to the issues teens face today.

For example, as I studied up on what interests teens—by talking to the teens I know, reading teen magazines and books, and using some of my own teenage experience—I realized that many young people (some even in their early teen years) are either already involved in a romantic relationship or are extremely interested in the subject of love and romance. Often, teens are confused by the subject of sex—to do or not to do—and many feel they can't talk to their parents about this concern.

When I wrote my book *Teen Astrology*, I was very aware of the importance of this topic and gave it a lot of thought and many pages of writing. Now that I am introducing another tool for self-knowledge, I want to address your specific needs for information. (Although you may have already read other Tarot books and may not be a complete novice, I have written this book as an introduction; I am assuming you have no previous knowledge of how to use the Tarot.)

Relationships of all kinds—not just romantic—are often uppermost in the minds of teens, to one degree or another. This includes your relationships with your parents, teachers, and other authority figures as well as your friends and peers. Many of you worry a lot about your relationships—especially when something isn't going well. Perhaps you are having love/romance/sex problems. Or you aren't getting along with your mother or father, or both!

Another frequent concern my teen friends tell me about is

that of social acceptance. Being liked and being popular are important to you. Feeling different, or being excluded or hassled just for being who you are, can be painful and make you feel wretched. Loneliness is another teen problem, especially if you have recently entered a new school or moved to a new location, leaving old friends behind. Making adjustments to these often upsetting conditions can be hard.

Of course, most teens are students; school and schoolwork take up a major part of your time. Making good grades isn't an issue for all teens, but for some—especially those whose parents have high expectations (sometimes too high!)—grades and testing can cause anxiety. Often, you like to know where you stand with your grades. Other concerns that come up on the teen screen are future educational choices, whether it's a good idea to take a year off before entering college, what course of studies to pursue, and career choices.

In delineating the interpretations for you, I've tried to take all of these considerations into account to help you deal with the inevitable challenges and frustrations, questions and upsets, that growing up entails. You will understand that it is just not possible to cover every single subject of concern to young people in a single book. But I've done my best to tailor the interpretations here so that you can use the Tarot as a *guide*. An old, popular saying is, "The unexamined life is not worth living." Using Tarot to examine your life as you go along living it day by day will give you an edge. It will help you to understand the forces at work in your life—both the external ones (about which sometimes you can do nothing) and the internal ones (which are really the most interesting). As a beginner, you will naturally have less experience both in life and in reading the Tarot, so I've tried to make the interpretations as simple and user-friendly as possible.

The Tarot Major Arcana can provide you with many insights into who you are and how you react to different situations—and

CONNECTING THE DOTS
Your entire life is a rich tapestry of meaningful connections, both inner and outer. *All* of the events in your life are connected by an intricate chain that involves your body, your experiences, your actions, your dreams, your hopes and wishes, and the contents of your daily thoughts. This complex web can best be understood symbolically. Using Tarot regularly hooks you into the language of symbols.

why you react the way you do. As I have stressed, everyone is an individual—unique, one-of-a-kind, with a life story different from everyone else's. You have a distinct personality and set of inner feelings. You have your own personal "blueprint" to follow. As you trod the path of the Tarot, you will appreciate your place in the complex web of energies and relationships that occur in every life. You'll see how past, present, and future relate to each other and unite all of humanity. Lastly, you will tap into the philosophical and metaphysical aspects of life, which can be a positive way of achieving valuable insights into your own and the general human condition.

Some religions forbid the use of what they call "occult" kinds of learning, and some people fear all forms of divination. However, this is mere superstition. If you are basically serious about the Tarot and have simple common sense and a positive attitude, there is absolutely nothing to fear from using it to get a peek into what the future *might* hold for you. If you use the Tarot as a teacher and a guide for self-knowledge—not as an infallible source of foretelling the future—it can do you no harm. Use of the Tarot for predictions is often called fortune-telling, a term that has unfortunate negative connotations. I prefer to regard predictions with wariness, taking them more as advice than as anything unchangeable, as I've said before.

Interpreting the Tarot for others is a very personal matter, an art, as opposed to anything scientific or concrete. Every reader will interpret from an individual point of view and, depending on experience, will be more or less helpful in telling what the cards "say." I've gotten many readings from others, and each one has been different, sometimes vastly so. We cannot avoid bringing our own particular attitude, philosophy, interests, and emotional coloration to our choice of interpretations. Because I am a psychotherapist, my "take" on a reading incorporates the inner state of the person; to my point of view, the cards often point out

THE SYMBOLIST PERSPECTIVE

The great American philosopher Ralph Waldo Emerson understood the value and importance of viewing one's entire life and surroundings symbolically. He said, "The whole world is an omen and a sign. Why look so wistfully in a corner? The voice of divination resounds everywhere and runs to waste unheard, unregarded, as the mountains echo with the bleatings of cattle."

the deep psychological issues that affect the practical problems of a situation.

Other factors that affect a reading are whether the reading is being done for oneself or for another person; and if for another person, that person's level of knowledge and maturity. For example, if I were reading for a seventeen-year-old, I'd approach the meanings of the cards differently than if I were reading for a seventy-year-old.

Teens will frequently want to read for other teens. Sharing readings is a good way to get acquainted with the cards, and experiencing the interpretive methods of friends who are also studying the Tarot broadens your own perceptions. Reading for others should not be undertaken as a parlor game. Approach your cards seriously and with respect. Working with the Tarot increases your opportunities to interact positively with others. When friends discover you are studying Tarot, they will probably ask for readings. This is okay, but always explain that you are only a student yourself. If you are normally somewhat reticent about making friends, or if you fear seeming foolish or not being accepted, the Tarot can help you overcome this block. Your peers will respect and even admire you for your ability with the cards. Of course, you don't want to read for anyone who is disdainful of the Tarot or other forms of divination.

Working with a friend or a group of friends on a regular basis is a good way to form bonds. Sit down together with the cards and share feelings about them and about the interpretations in a reading. You'll be surprised at how strong and positive these relationships will become. As you prepare for a reading by discussing what someone's question should be, you enter that person's private world, which increases your mutual rapport and promotes a psychic link between you for future readings.

This book focuses on meanings that are especially relevant to young people. However, because the Major Arcana are such

TEEN TAROT TIP
Reading for Others

When your friends learn you are studying Tarot, you'll surely be asked to read for them. This can be good practice if you bear in mind that in the psychic world there are always many variables. Today's situation may be different tomorrow. This applies especially to any negative cards. Be extremely careful about making firm pronouncements—there's going to be a lot you don't know, even about your own psyche and psychological makeup. The best course is prudence—speak of trends and possibilities, rather than making absolute statements that apply to the future. You'll appreciate the value of this approach, which will let you avoid creating any self-fulfilling prophecies, especially those indicating bad tidings. And choose your words with care—words are very powerful and need to be handled wisely.

rich, ancient archetypes, it's still necessary to pick and choose among numerous interpretations according to the age and stage of development both of yourself and anyone you read for. You may even want to read for adult members of your family—and that's good practice, too. Of course, when reading for an adult, you will choose interpretations that are appropriate.

As you continue to study and work with the cards of the Major Arcana, you'll get a feel for what is right in any given situation. You'll learn how to pose a question, either for yourself or for another. You'll get glimpses of future developments (on any level: practical, intuitive, or spiritual) and gain understanding of past events and how they affect current events or states of mind.

Remember that when using the Tarot's allegorical illustrations as a guide to your interpretations, you are interacting with a tradition that has its roots in the ancient world, a time when people were much more in touch with their intuitive faculties than they are in today's scientific-minded society, preoccupied as it is with rational thinking and technological advances. By studying standardized meanings, about which there is general agreement for the trumps, you release your own intuitive powers to pick the correct meaning for a particular question.

As you proceed through each of the cards of the Major Arcana one by one, as suggested previously, you will find that the images sink deep into your psyche, which allows your intuition to function remarkably well. This intuitive side of the art of interpretation is as important in the use of the Tarot as is study of specific meanings. (See my book *Your Psychic Potential* for a complete discussion, plus many helpful exercises, of how to develop your intuition.)

ANCIENT WISDOM, MODERN SCIENCE

"The decline of the symbolist worldview occurred in tandem with the advent of modern science in the seventeenth century. In recent decades, however, a series of important scientific theories have emerged which bear striking resemblance to key symbolist principles. Some writers have even gone as far as to suggest that science may be on the verge of explaining traditional symbolist notions."

Ray Grasse,
The Waking Dream

The Tarot is great for getting focused. I've noticed that quite a few young people aren't at all sure what course to follow. They can't make a decision about a career path, or they feel overwhelmed by the diverse options our culture offers. Yes, some people do take a long time to find their right path. But the decisions you make while young will affect what choices are still available when you're older. So choose carefully—and let the Tarot help you to envision your own future. Use it to examine a wide range of life's possibilities, to widen your horizons, and to explore what really sparks your enthusiasm and interest.

As you continue to work with the cards, be sure to use them for dream work. Choose a card and put it under your pillow at night. Get yourself acquainted with your own dreams for the future so that you can imagine yourself doing things you love. Get moving in the direction of your dreams now. Start investigating the pathways that lead to your desired future. When cards showing problems turn up, pay attention—these are important messages from you to yourself. Take a good look at the negative or problematic issues so that you can get a handle on them, make improvements, and take control of your destiny.

TEEN TAROT TIP

Always remember that the interpretation will be affected by the position of the card in the spread. Each position refers to a specific area of life, such as past influences or likely outcome.

We are such stuff
As dreams are made of
and our little life
Is rounded with a sleep.
William Shakespeare,
The Tempest

A Word about Reversed Cards

Some cards become reversed during the process of shuffling and mixing your deck. Opinion varies about reversed cards. I know readers who deliberately reverse cards by turning half of the deck opposite the other half when shuffling, but this seems contrived to me. I always begin the reading process with the entire deck of cards in the upright position. Then, if my reading person reverses cards while mixing or shuffling them, I accept them as reversed. But not always. Sometimes my intuition tells me that the card should be read right side up. Because many people are nervous when they come for a reading, it is common for a person to accidentally reverse half the deck, which can make for an entirely upside-down reading! So, feel free to choose how you want to interpret reversed cards, if at all. What you decide about this upright/reversed process is up to you. After studying the reversed meanings, if you want to experiment with reversed cards, it's another way to learn and to verify your intuition.

Reversed cards have just as many connotations as upright cards and can be difficult to understand—especially in the context of the whole reading. Some writers and readers like reversed cards because they double the number of possible interpretations. Such readers claim that several reversed cards in a single layout means multiple problems, which may not be the case. A little common sense is called for here. Are there just a few reversed cards in the deck when you begin reading, or are you turning up a slew of them? Remember, you are in charge of the reading and if your sense of the layout is that the reversed cards aren't right, turn them over. This is not to say that all reversed cards are negative, though that's the usual assumption. Some naturally negative cards, such as the suit of Swords, become more positive when reversed. Again, it's your decision to make. And you don't have to be consistent. Some layouts may feel just right even with reversed cards. Conversely, you may get an "all wrong" feeling. Also, it's important to read the reversed card in context with the entire spread. Look for the more positive cards as ways out of any difficulty indicated by reversed cards. As you are learning to trust your intuition, follow it where it leads!

O The Fool

Upright

When the Fool appears, you may be feeling "out of sync" with your life. Underneath you already know something needs to change—but what? You are being asked to take a risk, to do something on faith. Past experience may have made you wary of taking chances, but now's the time to put yourself to the test. You're still in a state of innocence. You may be a virgin. You could have just encountered your first love and be feeling unsure whether to take that leap. A new opportunity of some kind is indicated, if you are willing to take a chance. You seek adventure.

Reversed

You may fear making a fool of yourself, or be embarrassed about something you've done or not done. Fear of making a wrong choice is an issue. You feel a lack of opportunity for change, or a need to struggle against circumstances. There's risky business afoot. You are taking unnecessary chances for the sake of the thrill. Something is holding you back from going where you want to go. A new romance has gone sour. An inexperienced person is taking senseless risks. There's a possibility you're being duped. You took a chance and it backfired. Review the circumstances before acting.

I The Magician

Upright

It's time to take charge of your destiny. Learn to use the tools already at your disposal to better your life. New resources are available now. You want to be in control of things. You are studying hard to achieve. If romance is in the air, you are attracted to the right person. You are developing creative abilities, stretching yourself to the limit. You want to shape your own reality your way. Seek out opportunities by contacting the right people. Finding your true destiny. Being on a spiritual path. Someone is learning new and interesting things becoming an adept.

Reversed

Don't do anything rash. It's time to wait and see. You lack self-confidence or a strong sense of identity. You need to discover inner powers and resources independently. You are undecided about educational choices or need to do some self-searching to determine right goals. Develop a positive outlook on problems. You may have unrealistic romantic expectations. There's a rival for some desired outcome. You are not in a strong position now. Watch out for misuse of magical energy.

II The High Priestess

Upright

You are achieving a higher degree of self-awareness. Hidden inner things are becoming clear now. Your intuition is good; wisdom is developing. You want to penetrate to the heart of the matter. Keep your own counsel. You have secrets, or someone else is keeping a secret from you. A romantic situation requires more understanding. There are puzzles, factors of which you are unaware. Something is going to be revealed. You need insights into others' motivations. Partial knowledge is all that is available at this time.

This is a neophyte who is just learning the universal secrets. You are disappointed in love or unrealistic about romance. You're experiencing dreaminess and spaciness, wanting to be alone. You are questioning relations and other people's motives. You need to avoid people without spiritual ideals. Don't ask for more information about the situation than you can handle. You are not in harmony with your inner Self. Do a reality check on your relationships.

III The Empress

Upright

You are in the role of a nurturer or mother figure, perhaps to younger siblings. You have creative vision and social graces. If you are a girl, you are expressing your femininity positively. You take pride and pleasure in your sexuality and tend to your health properly. If you are a boy, the Empress represents your ideal woman. You have a good relationship with your mother, unless other negative cards in the spread say there are problems. The Empress can indicate passionate love and romance leading to a happy marriage and children. You or someone else may be thinking about marriage, motherhood, or pregnancy, a pregnancy that is wanted.

Reversed

You are lacking nurture. You're not getting mothered enough. You may have a bad or difficult relationship with your mother, or with a girl, if you are a boy. Someone is pressing you too hard for sex without a commitment. You may have an unwanted pregnancy. You are neglecting your health and bodily needs or trying to live up to unrealistic ideals of beauty. A boy might be looking for the "perfect" girl. You are dealing with human imperfection.

IV The Emperor

Upright

The Emperor can symbolize a good father or an authority figure in your life. Or you are attempting to become an authority figure for someone else or even for yourself. Young men may be seeking a father figure or a closer relationship with their father. You are dealing successfully with worldly issues, such as school or work. You may have a leadership position with much responsibility. Linear consciousness works well. You may have to take charge of a situation. Your self-confidence is high. Success, prosperity, status, and respect are promised if you play by the rules.

Reversed

You may be in conflict with the established order or be having problems with authority figures, especially your father. You may be dealing with an absent or negative father. You are questioning your traditional religion or ethnic base. Pressure to accept more responsibilities than you feel you can handle may be irksome. Fatigue is a problem, and lack of energy is holding you back. Your vitality is low—you might need a medical checkup.

V The Hierophant

Upright

This is an authority figure related to traditional religion or social status: a mentor, priest, or minister. It can describe a blessing from a higher authority. You might receive a recommendation for a scholarship or some award or grant. Your own internal spiritual voice is speaking out. You are engaged in higher education, possibly as a teacher yourself. Religious training may be in the cards. You might join a new religion. Traditions are important to you. You want to be a part of a larger whole, whether it is a religion, a philosophical point of view, a social organization, or some other type of group with authority. You are expanding spiritually.

Reversed

You are in revolt against your traditional religion. You have been turned down by a higher authority and are disappointed, maybe angry. Your behavior is offensive to those in authority, especially spiritual authority. You want to be your own conscience, not directed by others. You desire to develop your own code of ethics. You are intolerant of those on other spiritual paths. You are rebelling against restrictions such as school dress codes, customs, or institutional rules and regulations.

VI The Lovers

Upright

You are faced with a choice, possibly an important one. It may or may not have to do with love and romance, but it quite possibly is related to sexual activity. This choice may be the first you make independently of your parents. This card, in combination with other influential cards in the layout, will reveal qualities in yourself and another person that will affect your choice. Although the Lovers can refer to any significant choice, if sex is the issue, you must take into consideration your age and level of maturity, as well as the possible consequences, such as pregnancy and disease. Choose carefully! Another meaning is the melding of your own inner feminine and masculine characteristics.

Reversed

Indecision is a problem, or you have made an unwise choice and are now suffering the consequences. If a relationship is the issue, it might be abusive or troubled. You might have to choose whether to get out or stay. Counseling is advised. You're experiencing difficulties becoming your own person. Perhaps you're following the crowd instead of making meaningful choices based on your own needs and beliefs. You need more independence in making choices. You're relying too much on the approval of others.

VII The Chariot

Upright

Things are moving fast—perhaps faster than you'd like. You are in a period of rapidly occurring transition. You are working to hold things together and get your opposing energies harnessed to stay on track. Because you are completely, totally involved, and happily so, a good outcome is assured. You are getting it together with yourself and whatever needs to be accomplished. Keeping up a fast pace, you are in forward movement. Travel or relocating may be involved. You have to deal with personal affairs but you are attuned to the rhythm of it and keeping up with the changes that are happening. The Chariot foretells honors, successful endeavors, celebration, rewards for your efforts. You might be getting a new car or solving a transportation problem like how to get back and forth to school or a job. You are "in the driver's seat."

Reversed

Changes and transitions are happening internally at a rapid rate. You may feel that you are out of control, or that other people are controlling your life. You lack a sense of purpose and feel you are struggling to stay afloat. The pressure of being pulled in two directions at once, such as in a custody battle or family quarrel, may stress you out. It's a time to accept inner transition and make it positive. To do so, you must make an effort to get mental clarity about your direction in life. As you tune in to your own transition process, you will gain more control. You are having transportation problems, your car needs repair, or you can't get the use of your family vehicle.

(*Note:* Questions of transportation may seem trivial for a trump card, but in these days when a teen has to have "wheels" or a reliable source of transportation to get to school or a job, and to attend social functions, transportation is an important issue. The Chariot traditionally refers to modes of transport.)

VIII Strength

Upright

You are in a strong position, having weathered severe trials and triumphed. With your new-found deep inner strength, you are now "free to be" in a way you haven't been before. Because you are firmly grounded in the instinctual world, you can make friends with the lion and control its powers. When, at a gut level, you are connected positively to your animal self, it will protect and care for you. Body image is good now, and your attractiveness radiates from inside. Your inner drives are in harmony with your outer needs. You have the fortitude to accomplish what you want, especially in physical activities or athletics. If you have been ill, you will make a complete recovery. You can use your strength to help others and be a champion for them. It's a good time to build useful study habits and form healthy patterns of eating and exercise. Learn self-discipline through a practice combining physical, mental, and spiritual awareness, such as in the martial arts.

Reversed

You may be struggling with a bad body image or be out of sync with your physical and intuitive self. Your inner, instinctive nature is calling upon you to pay attention to your own needs—especially ones concerning your body and physicality, such as health and exercise. You may be feeling weak and unable to assert yourself in the situation. Your energy level may be erratic, your self-control at a low ebb. Although you are facing difficulties, you will eventually overcome them and come out on top. If your behavior seems illogical or contrary to what others—such as parents and friends—find normal or acceptable, it's because your basic survival instincts are warning you of danger to your integrity. You need to express yourself in ways that are more beneficial and true to your individuality.

IX The Hermit

Upright

The Hermit is a guide figure. It can refer to an older, wiser person or an inner guide who is nearby waiting for you to call on his wisdom or turn to him for advice. You may be actively seeking guidance from the invisible world. You feel a need to be alone for long periods to gain perspective on your life, and you are open to inner guidance. Although separation from others may be hard on some, time alone is necessary for the spiritual journey. You prefer the company of older persons at this time. You are on a quest for knowledge through devotion to your studies, turning to books such as this one for metaphysical information. Or you may be seeking an answer to some particularly difficult question about your life. Patience is called for. If the situation is knotty, you might go on a trip by yourself—perhaps into a wilderness retreat—to think things out and make a decision. It's possible you are looking for your own lost past.

Reversed

Are you putting off giving yourself the solitude you need to sort out your life and the issues you are currently confronting? The Hermit reversed suggests that you are staying extra busy to avoid what you really need to deal with. Your inner Guide is tapping at your door, knowing you need help, even though you are avoiding looking within. Are you fearful of what you will find there? If so, it's time—maybe long past time—for you to engage in some self-evaluation about your aims and goals, your friendships, your relationships, your career plans, your life path. You may be looking in all the wrong places for solutions to your problems. Or you may be mired in events of the past that were negative. You are in a sorting-out mode and need to get on with that process.

X The Wheel Of Fortune

Upright

Change is on the way. Prepare for the unexpected. Whatever happens, it's likely to be for the better, for you have put into motion an unstoppable course that will continue on of its own accord. You have done something—quit a job, entered or ended a relationship, joined or opted out of a group or activity—that has set a process in motion, and all will turn out as it is meant to. Just go with the flow. A new cycle is coming along, connecting you to your destiny. You may experience unexpected turns of events of the sort called synchronicity, such as a meeting with someone who helps you, receiving a beneficial offer, or being given a new opportunity or a second chance. These are part of the grand plan for your life. When the Wheel of Fortune turns, it is always the precursor of good fortune. Life is going your way. Take advantage of everything that shows up now.

Reversed

Are you holding back your own destiny by refusing necessary changes or required actions? If so, you are courting stagnation and frustration. You are bringing problems upon yourself by your foot-dragging. Change is inevitable. New cycles come into being when old ones end. Yes, it's uncomfortable; but standing still because you are fearful only makes things worse. Like it or not, change will come and you have to deal with it. You may think you are waiting for the "right" time, but fear of the unknown is undermining your future development. You are spending too much time fantasizing about what you want to do instead of steeling yourself to take the action necessary to get things moving again. Now is the time to send out a call to the Universe, asking to be shown the way. Fearlessly follow the direction you are given, even when there are delays or setbacks. Lack of commitment is a problem.

XI Justice

Upright

You may be involved with the law on some level—considering it as a career, seeking justice in personal matter, or being involved with a lawsuit. You are called on to work for fairness to everybody involved, to create a balance of power. Don't let your emotional reactions overtake your rational consideration. Stand firm and act with integrity and honesty, and all will be well. There may be an issue of the division of material possessions between you and others, such as with a legacy. Moderation and harmony will make relationships work. Be sure to take each individual's needs into consideration. Your judgment is sound; you may be called on to be an arbitrator because you are not swayed by personal considerations or bias. If a romantic relationship is at issue, remember that both partners deserve equal time and must have their needs recognized to achieve long-term success. You are against intolerance.

Reversed

You are experiencing delays—possibly in a legal matter—or unfairness in some situation, such as lack of recognition or losing your place on a team or in a group. Becoming angry and hostile will lead to defeat because you will be off balance or could possibly abuse your power. In a personal relationship, there is an inequality causing trouble, especially if one person is trying to exert power over the other. You may be festering with resentment over being treated unfairly; but sulking won't do the trick. The antidote is to become less dependent upon the outcome of events over which you have no control. There's always tomorrow. Do everything possible to avoid any conflict with the law. Your state of equilibrium is upset. If you are swinging from one extreme to another, you may need counseling to achieve a psychological balance.

XII The Hanged Man

Upright

You are in a state of suspension between options. You are viewing a problem from a new perspective. There is a pause between your regular activities and the future. You are faced with a choice among several directions. Spiritual growth is important now to form a firm foundation. You may be feeling the lack of power common to teens who are under the control of adults. You want to make your own decisions and be free of the restrictions resulting from being dependent on your parents, teachers, and other adults. This is the transitional state between being a child, or an adolescent, and being a grown-up. You are at a turning point and may feel lonely. Create your own rite of passage to ameliorate feelings of loneliness and ambiguity. You are in a state of formation, like the caterpillar in its chrysalis. Soon you will emerge into your own light.

Reversed

Your life is at a standstill and you can't seem to move forward. You feel stuck and unable to effect change. Everyday concerns may seem overwhelming. You're tired of waiting and want action but are blocked. You may have to make a sacrifice—or to stop making sacrifices and concentrate on your own development. You want personal independence but feel pulled back to being dependent. You are resisting your own necessary growth, perhaps out of fear of failure. You feel your life is "on hold" while you wait for the time you can be on your own. Patience is needed. Change will come. You will move forward in time. Hang in there!

XIII Death

Upright

The Death card does *not* portend real physical death. It is actually a positive card because it indicates a transformation for the better, the end of the old, outworn thoughts and circumstances that are preventing new development. A dramatic change in your consciousness is predicted—you are being regenerated at a deep level and superficial changes won't cut it. Instinctively you know this, but you may be afraid. You may feel everything is falling apart, especially your sense of personal identity. But you are in the process of creating a new, fuller identity more in sync with who you truly are. Whatever is no longer necessary—a love relationship, bad habits, negative thoughts, certain friendships—must "die" to make room for that which is more desirable and will work better for you. A new cycle is coming into being. Accept this as part of life's process. You may be ending something—let go of attachments that no longer serve your real needs. If you are preoccupied with thoughts of death—*especially if you think of suicide*—get help from a counselor.

Reversed

Someone you know may be dying, but this is unlikely unless an elderly, sick person is involved. You may yourself have had a brush with death—an automobile or other type of accident. Fear of death may be oppressing you. You have to confront your fears and overcome them, realize that death is a natural part of life. Also, the passing of the old—whether a stage of life, an activity, or certain relationships—is a necessary precursor to the new, which is always better because it represents growth. Without growth, we do die. Depression may be an issue. If so, consult a responsible adult and get help. You may have suffered a painful loss—of a pet, a friend, a familiar way of life—that has affected you deeply. Look to positive cards in the spread for ways of coping with your pain.

"At every moment we are dying and renewing ourselves. Each moment we see that a new consciousness, a new thought, a new hope, a new light is dawning in us. When something new dawns, at that time, we see that the old has been transformed into something higher, deeper, and more profound."

Sri Chinmoy,
Death and Reincarnation: Eternity's Voyage

XIV Temperance

Upright

You are learning to blend the opposites in your life—schoolwork and play, material and spiritual concerns, activities and the need for rest and relaxation, your own inner masculine and feminine qualities. You are in a state of experimentation, mixing together the different streams of your consciousness and unconsciousness. You are creating harmony in your daily life and finding creative outlets for your imagination and for problem solving. Moderation is called for in all things now. Don't overdo or overreact. Take time to meditate and reflect. Strive to achieve balance. Your health is good or will improve. It's a good time to take up practices such as yoga or tai chi, which balance the body, mind, and spirit. As you achieve the correct balance of the many facets of your life—school and studying, friends and peers, parents and authority figures, love and romance relationships, sports and other extracurricular activities, you will find harmony and peace. A guardian angel is near.

Reversed

What was working before has stopped being effective. You are out of balance. Outward circumstances may be chaotic or out of control. You are struggling with everyday matters more than usual. Creative projects aren't going well and you feel discouraged and lack confidence in your abilities. You may feel inferior or aware of an inequality in a relationship or situation. Ask your guardian angel for guidance and you will receive it—but only if you are open to the message you get. You may be ill—physically or psychologically—and depressed about how you feel. If your condition is serious, be sure to get help. Sometimes just talking to a responsible, caring adult will permit you to get a new perspective and rebalance what is out of whack. Readjustments are important now. Get feedback from someone you trust. Look to other cards for clues.

XV The Devil

Upright

The Devil card represents the bondage we create and maintain ourselves. Ask yourself: What is limiting me and how am I responsible for the situation? Is my behavior self-defeating? What can I do to change it? Beware of addictions or risky behavior that may lead to them or other trouble—or there'll be "the devil to pay." Obstacles may be frustrating, options limited. Others may be involved, but *you* have the choice to free yourself. Note that the chains on the people on this card are loose and could be slipped off. We all face limitations on our freedom of action, and teens often respond to these restrictions by rebellion or compulsive behaviors. You may be doing things you don't really want to do—going along with the crowd while knowing you're doing something destructive. Or maybe you're totally in thrall to the material world of possessions and status that is often the root of a problem. Remember that you *always* have choices, even if only in how you choose to react to a bad situation. Sexuality may be an issue that you need to address in a mature way without being impulsive or allowing yourself to feel pressured. Just tell others to back off if you want to stay in control of yourself.

Reversed

You feel trapped. Maybe you've been grounded. Tension is high, possibly because of sexual pressures. You may be struggling with an addiction or have a family member who is addicted and causing you grief. If there are hidden resentments, you need to bring them out into the open to avoid a hostile confrontation. There is a potential for things going wrong. Friends and peers may seem like they're "out to get you," and this can cause feelings of paranoia. Talk to a responsible adult if you are fearful or being abused by *anyone* at all. You have nothing to fear but fear itself. If you are seriously depressed, get counseling.

XVI The Tower

Upright

The Tower represents disruption or adversity that destroys or overthrows false ideas and old habit patterns. However, it is *not* a negative card but a positive one, because it symbolizes creative breakthroughs and insights into knotty problems. You may experience a lightning flash of insight—the "bolt from the blue" that makes everything come clear. However, since many teens find anything that upsets their regular routine to be threatening, it can engender distinctly uncomfortable feelings. Nevertheless, what is destroyed has served its purpose and needs to go. The Tower seems to turn up when a person has become stuck, unsatisfied, and discontent, but doesn't know how to change things. If a relationship is at issue, the two people may be temperamentally volatile and, like a simmering volcano, sooner or later there is an eruption. You might be deeply involved in a family quarrel or feeling the effects of some other kind of disruption like a family move to a new location, or having to attend a new school. Whatever the situation you face, it is firing an urgent need to break free of restrictions that limiting your further development.

Reversed

An accident is a real possibility, so take great care driving, using fire, power tools, or performing sports. Emotions may be at a high pitch, ready to explode, especially if there has been a period of frustration. Let off steam safely. Don't let hostile emotions build to the breaking point. Avoid any confrontation with the law. Don't give anyone in authority "attitude." Stay calm and collected. Inner emotional turmoil may be causing physical illness. See a physician if you feel sick. Avoid bad company. Accept that disruption is a signal that something is not right and needs to be changed.

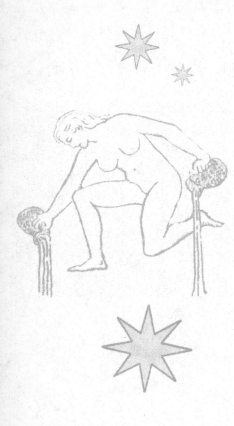

XVII The Star

Upright

You are at a significant turning point. You are experiencing a new flow of energy and self-confidence. Assistance is coming your way, both from the invisible world and the material world. As you flow with the pure energy of the Universe, you are realizing your place in it, intuiting a special destiny sure of fulfillment. Trust in life and its many processes; set goals for the future. Your creativity is at a high point and you are opening to new opportunities. You feel good about yourself. Now is the time to concentrate on developing all your various talents, seeking out what's inside you waiting to be developed. Fate is on your side because you are in harmony with the Universe and its purposes. Expect benefits from the material world in the form of money, possessions, recognition, or assistance—like financial support for college or a recommendation for a job or special course of study. The Star also means that the question relates to your soul life and spiritual aspirations, and it promises spiritual guidance.

Reversed

You are having a difficult time sustaining your spiritual goals. Creatively, you feel blocked, but this is temporary. Maybe you aren't ready yet for what you want to achieve. You may be failing to make the most of yourself because your outer ambitions are not in line with your inner heart's desire. You may be recovering from some traumatic experience, a slow process with many frustrations. Be patient. Things will come right in time. Seek out spiritual guidance from those who can help you grow and develop. Look inward for insights to your problem. Deliberately open yourself up to receiving angelic support and guidance.

XVIII The Moon

Upright

The Moon deals with the lunar realm of instincts, dreams, intuition, poetry, and inspiration. You may be in a mysterious process of shapeshifting—entering puberty or embarking on sexual activity. As these changes are inner as well as outer, they may be confusing you or making you feel uptight. Change is difficult for everyone, especially for teens who are in an intense state of change all the time, both hormonally and psychologically. You are becoming more aware of your inner nature, of the multiple and subtle shadings and nuances of feelings. The Moon highlights creative imagination. Fantasy is enjoyable and can lead to self-knowledge. It can indicate psychic development, letting you tune in more accurately to the vibrations of others. As the Moon heightens emotions—especially of the dreamy, romantic kind— you may be "mooning" over someone, possible an unavailable someone such as a celebrity. There's a quality of illusion here, but that's okay, it's how we learn—by trying on various personalities and seeing how they fit. Just don't go too far and become immersed in an impossible dream.

Reversed

You may be cutting yourself off from your inner Self. Or perhaps you've been told that your desire for artistic creation, for lingering with your dreams, or for spending time alone, is a bad thing, or that you should be more productive; and so you are feeling guilty about your Moon needs. Daily demands are overwhelming. You need time out to contact your inner lunar self, either through communing with Nature or allowing yourself to drift and dream awhile. This will help open the channel through which the divine Goddess energy flows. By putting more "soul time" into your life, you will find a softer, gentler way of dealing with the sometimes stringent requirements of the daily grind.

XIX The Sun

Upright

The Sun symbolizes energy, vitality, confidence, success, and good times. This powerful, positive card can offset any negative cards in the same spread. The Sun represents children and childhood as well as creativity and pleasure. You are feeling the wonder of it all the same way a child does, experiencing new beginnings, a sense of well-being, of accomplishment, success, contentment. Your optimistic and happy frame of mind is contagious, so you make friends readily. Cheerful and self-confident, you are full of life and vitality, ready to take on just about anything and everything. Your enthusiasm is so high that you aren't worried about the outcome. You may be starting several new projects, or upgrading something—your computer, your car, your room. You may visit or move to a sunnier location, which you'll like.

Reversed

Even reversed, the Sun is never a negative card. However, there will be delays, and you will have to make some adjustments or alterations to plans or projects. But that's no sweat. Your confidence is high—you may need to tone it down a bit to keep things on an even keel—but you feel fine just the way you are. Circumstances are requiring you to make some minor changes, though. You might need to spruce up your appearance for that interview with the college administrator or work harder at developing your talents. It's important that you find new and more effective ways to express who you are to the outside world now, because you want to put your best foot forward in all situations.

XX Judgment

Upright

This card signals a wake-up call from the Universe telling you it's time for a new phase of your maturing process. It's also a sign that you are growing in awareness of how Spirit is incorporated into everyday life. A new phase of your life is beginning. You are like a tree that has gone through the process of growing roots, making leaves, budding, and flowering, and is now ready to produce fruit. You need to let yourself grow and mature at a steady pace. Don't try to rush the process. You might be graduating from one level of school to another, or making other significant changes. These might involve so-called rites of passage, celebrations or rituals that mark a transition from one stage of life to the next. Decisions are important now, for they will be far-reaching. Some people may be judging you—for example, school examiners or possible employers. You could receive some public recognition. New directions, opportunities, interests, enthusiasm—all are distinct possibilities now.

Reversed

You aren't there yet, but you feel ready to think about changes. Then again, you may be resisting the idea of change. Things are moving more slowly than you'd like. Nonetheless, you are coming into a new phase in your life and, like it or not, you must deal with it. Indecision may be a problem. Ego is getting in the way of judgment. Emotionally, you are being called upon to grow up, and you may find that scary. You do not want to face reality. Other possible meanings that may apply are these: you need an attitude adjustment; complications and frustrating delays are thwarting you; you dislike or disagree with others' judgments of you; you've had a loss or separation and need to cope with the resulting life changes; a life-transforming experience is in the works.

XXI The World

Upright

Oh, happy day! The world is your oyster. You are pointing toward a successful career or rewarding course of action. You feel in control of your life and you are expressing yourself well. Everything is going your way. Self-development is at the fore now. You are in a stage of completion—you are meeting your goals, developing your potentials, and are on the way to achieving your most cherished aims. Success, happiness, harmony: all are assured. An old cycle has ended and a new one begun. You are sure of your life path. Whatever you undertake now will come to fruition, in harmony with your world. The quality of your home life, your school and/or work environment, and your natural surroundings will all play a role. Supported by your inner resources, you are the master of your soul. You are enjoying supreme self-confidence and hope of victory. Having put your trust in the Higher Power, you will receive the rewards due you, as you can now manifest good things in your life through your own positive thoughts and actions. Many opportunities are available to you. You have earned the right to choose what pleases you and make it work well.

Reversed

Your world has been turned upside down, either because your goals are not in harmony with your inner needs or because you are preoccupied with material success and are neglecting your spiritual life. You need to ask yourself if the course of action you are planning is the right one for who you are. Then you need to find the right place, the right people, and the right situation. You have a wide variety of choices and aren't sure which one to make. It's time to investigate your spiritual nature in relation to how you deal with the material world. There are different levels of reality, and you need to recognize this. You may be rejecting opportunities out of fear or a materialistic view of life.

Tarot Play Exercise

GETTING TO KNOW THE TRUMPS

Separate the Major Arcana cards from the rest of the cards in your deck and do a reading with them only. (See Chapter 13 on spreads.) Pick a simple layout, one with three, five, or six cards. Ask a verifiable question, one for which you can ascertain whether your interpretations were correct within a fairly short time—two weeks at most. For example, you could ask the likely outcome of a sports event, a blind date, a school contest, or an exam.

Draw the layout you use in your Tarot notebook and note the name of the card in each position in the spread. Then make your interpretations. Include your overall assessment of the outcome, based on your question. After the event in question has come to pass, go back to your notebook and check up on your interpretations. How close did you come? Were you right on the mark, or totally off base?

With this information, you can assess the quality of your interpretations. If you were mostly correct, congratulate yourself—you are hooked up with your intuitive processes. If you were way off, ask how you could have interpreted the cards differently. Consider how you posed the question, too. Asking the right question leads to getting the right answer.

You can do this play exercise as many times as you like. It's a good way to get to know your trump cards intimately and also to keep tabs on your progress with interpretations.

If you are puzzled about a particular card in a spread, or if you are doing a verification exercise and can't figure out what went wrong, shuffle the deck thoroughly and then go through it until you find the card you want to know more about. See which cards turn up on either side of the card you are questioning. These will throw light on the matter.

The Minor Arcana

Evidence suggests that the Minor Arcana were linked up with the Major Arcana sometime in the fourteenth or fifteenth centuries, and that they originally were used both as playing cards and for fortune-telling. There are no standardized symbolic meanings for the Minor Arcana, as there are for the Major Arcana. Therefore, interpretations vary. Some who write about the Tarot concentrate on the Major Arcana and virtually ignore the Minor Arcana, while others use a primarily numerological approach, since most of the cards are number cards.

STRUCTURE OF THE MINOR ARCANA

The Minor Arcana are set up like a deck of ordinary playing cards, with four suits, in this case, Wands, Pentacles, Swords, and Cups. Each suit has fourteen cards: ten number cards and four court cards (King, Queen, Knight, and Page). We'll take an introductory look at all these components now, so you can begin to see how the numbers, court cards, and suits fall into useful categories. Then, in the following chapters, we'll examine each component from every which way until you've got a working knowledge of every card in the deck.

Let's begin with the number cards. The ten number cards of each suit, starting with Ace and going up to Ten, are called the *pip* cards. Pips are the dots or markings on each number card that denote that card's numerical value. The pip cards have no spiritual or teaching qualities, and in some decks are not illustrated at all, the pips being merely decorative. Pip cards generally refer to the ordinary, routine events and emotions of daily life. Occasionally, they will describe personal characteristics either of the reader or someone involved in the situation. As a rule of thumb, pip cards are about situations or emotions currently happening or about to happen.

Although pip cards are illustrated in many different ways, the illustrations have no specific relationship to the number, which is the important quality of the pips. In many decks, pip cards carry no pictures at all but are merely stylized in accordance with their suit symbol. For example, the Four of Wands may be just four Wands arranged attractively on the card.

A major exception is the Waite deck, in which each pip card depicts a person or people performing a definite activity. Unfortunately, these illustrations can cause confusion in interpretation. Sometimes the illustration contradicts the overall meaning of the suit involved and makes no specific reference to the numerological meaning.

It has been speculated that the pip cards were given illustrations as a memory tool, especially in the case of the Waite deck, upon which many other modern decks have been based. True enough, the Waite deck's illustrations stick in the mind. For example, the vivid illustration of nine Swords lined up over the head of a young woman sitting up in bed holding her head in her hands as if just awakened from a horrible nightmare is unforgettable.

ANCIENT NUMEROLOGY

The study of the significance of numbers as symbols has a long history. Some ancient peoples thought that the world was created on the basis of numbers. The great Greek philosopher Pythagoras, who gave the world his famous geometry in the sixth century B.C.E., held that numbers were the essence of Being. Pythagoras is known for his discovery that the musical scale can be expressed in mathematical ratios. He based this idea on something called "the music of the spheres," supposing that as the celestial bodies travel through space they produce music. The theories of Pythagoras form the basis for Western astrology and its "aspects," or planetary relationships. Thus, his numerical system has become the basis for many Western divinatory practices, including astrology and the Tarot.

Although five hundred years' worth of Tarot interpretations has produced some agreement on the significance of the Minor Arcana cards, the agreement is not universal. Therefore, I think it's best to stick to basing interpretations of the pip cards on the meaning of the number itself, about which there *is* general agreement. However, I will say that sometimes my intuition hooks into the picture and it reveals something useful. Because interpretation is an art, not an exact science, you need to be aware of the possibilities inherent in the deck you are using and your own intuitive process regarding the cards in general or a particular reading.

The student of Tarot needs to have a working knowledge of numerology to interpret the pip cards. It's best to learn the basic meanings of the ten numbers (Ace to Ten) and review them frequently. As you use your cards you will get more and more familiar with the numbers and their meanings until they become second nature. (We will discuss the meanings of the numbers in Chapter 8.)

Now, about the court cards: In most decks, the court cards are similar in design to those on ordinary playing cards, though the illustrations for the King, Queen, Knight, and Page might have some variations among the different suits. Often the designs will depend on the philosophical point of view of the designer; some are entirely plain, so that the only way to tell the difference between the suits is to look for the suit symbol on the card, or a label at the bottom of the card.

Again, the Waite deck is an exception to this general rule. In it, the Wands, Pentacles, Swords, and Cups are worked right into the illustrations. I find the court cards in the Waite deck to be excellent representations both of the nature of each suit and of the specific meaning of each court figure. For example, the Queen of Cups is a lovely figure gazing at a large cup as if she might read the future in its contents. She represents creativity and otherworldliness. In contrast, the King of Swords holds his sword upright as if about to use it. He signifies either spiritual advance or cutting through obstacles.

SIGNIFICANCE OF THE MINOR ARCANA

The primary function of the Minor Arcana is to relate to the every-day world—with all of its variables, trials and tribulations, successes and joys. The Minor Arcana cards can be extraordinarily accurate for questions about the here and now, because they refer to specific areas of human experience. While there is in them no actual reference to spiritual growth, each of the life areas to which they apply can certainly be approached as part of one's spiritual development. For example, the Cups refer to relationships, the Wands to personal growth. From this point of view, we can say there is nothing without its spiritual significance. Every action of every day can be cause for spiritual celebration, as I have written extensively about in my book *Awaken to Your Spiritual Self.*

In order to grasp the significance of the Minor Arcana, it's important to understand them as a sort of commentary on the Major Arcana, within the context of the reading. There is no need to search for any mystical meaning to attach to them. However, don't come to the conclusion that by themselves they have no real significance. The numerological references of the pip cards can be extremely useful, but they must be integrated into the context of each reading. After you've read the next chapter and you understand a bit about numerology, you will find that they are full of significance relating to the specific question for which the Tarot is being consulted.

YOUR SACRED SELF

"And in truth, the divine is everywhere. We have only to look and listen. Most magnificently, the sacred is inside each of us, nestled in the most interior part of our beings. Alas, our perception of the sacred within ourselves and all around us is too often buried beneath an encrustation of the demands and expectations of others—family, teachers, society and its institutions, which serve to obscure our ability to realize and recognize the divine spirit glowing within ourselves. But no matter how faint the ember, we have only to go deeply within to find its eternal spark and fan it into new and vibrant life. The Light is always there.

To know one's self deeply and intimately is to know the divine spirit."

M. J. Abadie,
Awaken to Your Spiritual Self

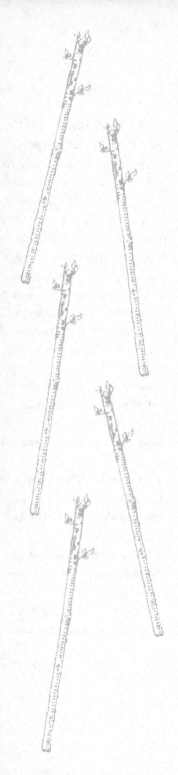

THE FOUR SUITS

In medieval times, the four suits of the Minor Arcana were identified with the four main classes into which people were divided—the nobility, the clergy, the merchant class, and the working class. Though technically today these "classes" have changed form, our modern society still shows vestiges of them. You could say that the elite, old money class is our version of nobility; scientists, professionals, and academies make up our clergy category; corporations now populate our merchant class; and "blue collar" workers are the current working class.

The Wands

According to tradition, the Wands relate to the idea of life and growth. They are also called Scepters, Batons, Rods, Clubs, and Staves. These terms refer to action, often work that involves competition and commerce. When Wands appear, it is an indication that the person is actively working on self-confidence and identity development, especially with a young person who is still in the process of acquiring these qualities. Related to the element Fire, Wands indicate energy, self-confidence, and the ability to approach problems creatively. Reversed Wands may be a sign that you are dealing with stress caused by overactivity or too intense competition. Wands often show an entrepreneurial disposition in the person.

Wands also pertain to the outside world where, usually, work takes place. In readings for teens, they often point to the ways teens express themselves through projects, sports and recreation, social activities, scholastic matters, and achievements in general.

Teenagers express Wands energy in a variety of ways—through making plans for future work, actually having a part-time job, interacting with people outside the framework of home and school, going on outdoors adventures, and taking on creative projects either for school or in the family. An especially important way teens use Wands energy is in active, competitive situations like sports, games, or other extracurricular activities. Some other Wands-powered actions teens go for are field trips, career investigations, self-started small enterprises that make money, and interactions with the public, through service work or volunteering.

Young people are constantly exploring in an effort to find their identities, trying on different personalities so to speak—ways of dressing and behaving—and the Wands cards speak to this process directly. Lots of Wands in a reading can point out someone who is a self-starter, has initiative, is a leader, is motivated, and enjoys being out in the world with people.

The Wands show action in progress or about to happen. Things can happen quickly when Wands are prominent in a reading. The various Wands cards will spell opportunities for work, adventure, travel, or some combination of these. With Wands, life is interesting, and new people are likely to come along and enliven things. With Wands, you'll have enthusiasm and eagerness to exchange ideas and find new ways of expression.

The Pentacles

The Pentacles, also called Coins or Disks, are related to money, security, financial resources, social status, goods and possessions, and the physical and material world in general. The element is Earth. The Pentacle is a magical symbol. Most Tarot decks show them as coin-shaped and inscribed with a pentagram (a five-pointed star). Pentacles show a focus on the use of the five senses, or the strictly material side of reality, and the use of rational thought to understand the material world.

When Pentacles turn up in a teen's reading, that teen usually has issues around money and how to get more of it. He or she is concerned about practical matters—where to live, how to make a living, how to allot one's resources, including money and time.

Pentacles stand for the physical side of life, including health and physical needs, being responsible for material goods, planning for the future realistically, and creating a place in society.

Teenagers are likely to face Pentacles issues frequently, as there is always pressure to focus on studies and get good grades so you can either get into the right college or get a well-paid job after high school. Pentacles refer to family obligations, practical goals, learning job skills, entering the work world, and learning how to handle money independently of parents. Money is often a primary issue for teens—how to earn it, spend it, or save it up. Reversed Pentacles can hint at a shortage of money, or fear of losing what you have. Many teens are addicted to acquiring material possessions; reversed Pentacles can be a signal that you have gone too far in one direction and need to consider other values. Reversed Pentacles can warn of rigid thought patterns, materialism, greed, snobbery, being judgmental, considering money as a god.

With Pentacles showing in your spread, you have probably achieved some solid accomplishments on which to build your future. You may be developing management skills either through study or a part-time job. Confidence in problem solving is good when you can get hard facts and deal with the "real world" in a concrete way.

Pentacles energy doesn't go in for daydreaming or artistic imagination, but it can invite you to take up craftwork, woodwork, or some other hands-on hobby or career. Pentacles energy likes to be able to see, touch, hold, smell, and hear results. Some Pentacles, such as the Three, indicate real craftsmanship or mastery of a practical skill. Others suggest learning new skills, becoming an apprentice, or doing something requiring hands-on labor. There is usually a period of trial and error before mastery is gained.

The Swords

The Swords are related to Self and the obstacles the Self faces. The element is Air. In medieval times, Swords represented the absolute rule of a sovereign, enforced by the power of the sword. At the same time, the rulers were aware of their obligations to the people—the obligation to better the lives of those under their control.

Thus, the Swords have a dual quality. They have come to symbolize negativity, such things as anxiety, depression, pain, violence, hatred, and enemies. Yet they point to the noblest qualities of which humans are capable and therefore they carry a spiritual connotation. For example, the Ace of Swords indicates the beginning of a new spiritual path. The trials and tribulations represented by the Swords lead to the development of character.

The domain of the Swords being mental in nature, Swords often refer to states of mind rather than outside conditions. These can be positive or negative: ideas and abstract thinking, or despair and anxiety. The colors of the cards often suggest the moods of the person. There's also an implication of who has and who has not got the power in a given situation. There can be a reference to matters involving religion, philosophy, politics, and the institutions that support these social functions, like school and church, news media, political parties, and other social and religious groups. The source of power in a society or an individual life may derive from adherence to a particular ideology.

Young people are almost always being confronted with issues of power—in school, in the family, in extracurricular activities such as athletics, and in peer groups. Teens tend to experience the energy of Swords when they are involved in defending their ideas or their personal space. The appearance of Swords often means worry, trying to solve problems (often alone, without adult help or guidance), feeling lonely or abandoned, deprived or left out, coping with loss or heartache—especially if a romantic situation is the

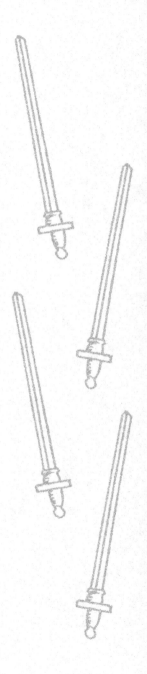

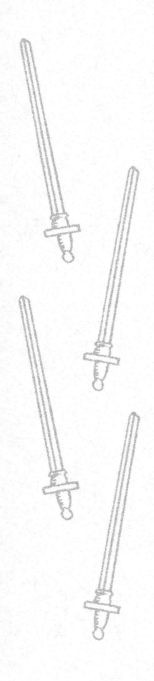

issue. Swords point to teens' disagreement (usually with parents, occasionally siblings) about lifestyles and privileges, about who's in charge of what. A teen may be struggling with questions of ethics or morals, concerned about the opinions of others (especially authority figures), be unsure how to behave in a particular situation, or be dealing with aggression or tough competition. Abuse of some sort is also a possibility to consider.

What Swords are doing when they turn up in a reading is asking you to tap into your powers of discernment, to make decisions based not on your emotions but on your reasoning power. You may be so enmeshed in the emotion—be it negative (that's usual) or positive—that you are having trouble sorting out the wheat from the chaff. What you need is a more realistic outlook, which can be difficult to achieve when you are in a state of heightened emotional stress and feeling fear, anxiety, or depression.

You need to get some distance from the situation. Step back a few paces and try to see things clearly. Emotions make the mind murky. Use a discrimination process to set things straight, to get clear about what is illusion and what is reality, and to understand just how your own mental patterns and habits are affecting you at the time. It's not easy to solve Swords-type problems, but when you work to find a solution that takes everyone into consideration, you are likely to be successful. Look to other, positive cards in the spread for clues about problem solving. Always moderate any aggressive feelings with clear thinking, and never take aggressive action to solve a problem.

Life has its limitations, and the Swords speak to this reality. The best way to solve a Swords problem is to assess the problem realistically and accept that there are always restrictions on your freedom of action. Destructiveness never works for long and always causes more trouble. There's a term for the person who can handle Sword problems well—this person is a *spiritual warrior,* someone who understands that the main struggle is with the Self.

The Cups

The Cups are related to emotions, love, romance, the unconscious, and creativity. Their association is with the clergy of medieval times, who were second only to the nobility in influence in the society. The local priests used available resources to alleviate the sufferings of their flock. Thus, the Cups came to represent love, harmony, good faith, and benevolent influences. They sometimes refer to romantic love. Because cups are containers, they are symbols of what is feminine and receptive, of nurture and creative or idealistic fulfillment. The element is Water. Cups speak about emotions and the constant flux of feelings.

Since teens are usually in a state of some sort of emotional arousal, the Cups often turn up in their readings. They hint at dreams and dreamy states of mind, murky moods, vague feelings, and the inner world. Cups also point to creativity or special gifts of psychic power or intuition. Almost always positive, Cups symbolize all that nourishes the creative spirit. If you get several Cups in a reading, chances are you have artistic leanings you need to pay attention to.

Cups are also about the everyday comforts of life—good food, a comfortable environment, social pleasures, emotional peace, small blessings. You may be in a situation of nurturing someone else, or be taking care of a loved pet. Whatever the issue, it will be around feelings, possibly intense ones. The Cups describe unconscious processes, and as a teen you are in the process of having your unconscious self awakened—sexually, emotionally, creatively, spiritually. You may be yearning for the ideal love relationship or attempting to figure out what love is. With Cups, the emphasis is always on expressions of love and your inner life. A reading with many Cups declares your readiness to develop your emotional responses in depth, your ability to have a sure sense of identity as a person with feelings that are to be respected. Your soul needs are calling to you.

THE COURT CARDS

The royal court of the Tarot consists of a King, a Queen, a Knight (usually on horseback), and a Page. The court cards have two basic functions: one is to represent different aspects of yourself that apply to the situation; the other is to represent the people active in your life during the time of the reading. Here's a brief rundown of the aspects of the court cards:

❖ Facets of your personality that you are expressing

❖ Qualities you are trying to develop

❖ Your current sense of identity, or a role you are playing

❖ Specific people in your life

Reversed court cards can personify actual people who are obstacles or somehow problematic. Or they can personify negative use of your own personal qualities.

When several court cards turn up in a single reading, it suggests that your question or situation involves several other people. For example, a King, a Queen, and a Page in the same spread might represent your father, your mother, and yourself as the young person.

One way to identify a court card with a person is astrologically. The Wands represent fire signs (Aries, Leo, Sagittarius). The Swords represent air signs (Gemini, Libra, Aquarius). The Pentacles represent earth signs (Taurus, Virgo, Capricorn). The Cups represent water signs (Cancer, Scorpio, Pisces). Since you know your own sign and probably the Signs of most of your friends, parents, and relatives, you can make a fair judgment based on that. For example, if your mother is an earth sign and the Queen of Pentacles comes up, it's likely to be her. And so on.

Another way to assign the court cards to people is by their physical characteristics. Wands represent people who are red-haired or reddish blonde and have light or fair skin, with hazel or brown eyes. Cups represent people who are light haired (blonde, light brown, gray) and have light or medium-toned skin, with blue, gray, or hazel eyes. Swords represent people who are swarthy, with olive or medium-toned skin, dark brown or black hair, and light-colored eyes. Pentacles represent people who are dark-haired and have dark or sallow skin, with brown or black eyes.

These descriptions are only general indicators. Your Capricorn mother may have medium-brown hair and hazel eyes and still fit the Queen of Pentacles. The King of Swords could represent your Aquarius father, even if his skin is light and eyes brown. It's not an either/or proposition, but one of using your judgment. As a personal example, I find that I often turn up in my clients' readings as the Queen of Pentacles. I have fair skin and blonde hair—but I'm a Capricorn and she fits my personality. However, I can also be represented by the Queen of Swords or Cups in different contexts. The same variations will be true of which court cards represent which people in your life, and this may change with changing situations and questions.

You can also use the court cards as significators. (See the discussion of significators in chapter 5 and the box in chapter 8.) Briefly, Kings and Queens represent mature adults, often a teenager's parents or teachers, usually over the age of forty, but possibly also a younger person who is exceptionally mature for his or her age (as the earth signs often are). Knights represent adults from about twenty to forty, but might also represent an older person who carries age lightly. Pages represent very young adults, teens, and children. However, an adult with childlike qualities—say, someone who is artistic, creative, and full of wonder—may call forth a Page figure. As usual, you have to be creative in your interpretations and in matching up the Court cards to actual persons.

Many times, the sex shown on the card will be the gender of the person. However, though the illustrations almost always show Knights as men, they may also represent women. The Pages, too, are most often shown as young boys, but can just as well be any young person, especially a teen, of either sex. What is important is that the match you make fits your impressions.

Kings

Kings are often fathers in a teen's reading, or male authority figures like teachers or religious leaders. However, they can also stand for characteristics that you yourself possess, such qualities as leadership, initiative, a sense of being in command of yourself, entrepreneurial tendencies, a take-charge personality, or high status in your school or peer group. Kings point to effective action, ethical principles, and the ability to get things done efficiently. They can also be expressions of public life—recognition, awards, honors, trophies, publicity, public celebrations or events, political activities. They are unlikely to signify specific situations.

Queens

Queens are often mothers, motherly women, or teachers in a teen's reading. A Queen can represent any mature woman, but she is usually a strong woman with some kind of authority or a powerful personality. Queens can also represent your personal characteristics, whether you are male or female, though in my experience Queens and Kings usually correlate to the sex of the person. A young girl who is "queening it" may be exhibiting the negative characteristics of a Queen; this typical Leo trait is not reserved to that sign but applies across the zodiac to anyone who is giving oneself airs. It is possible for Queens to represent adult males who have nurturing qualities like helpfulness, kindness to children and animals, and so forth.

Knights

Knights in a teen's reading usually represent sons or possibly siblings. They bring action into the picture, revealing that something is about to happen. Knights show that new experiences and new people are coming into your life soon. There may be much coming and going around you when Knights appear, or you may be feeling restless and in need of action yourself. There's a sense of gearing up for "battle" of some sort—you might be entering an athletic or other type of competition that requires a high level of energy, strength, courage, and adaptability. Your drive is in fast gear and you are ready to face challenges, come what may. Knights can represent the late teen years, or the transfer from high school into college or the work force. When a Knight appears, it is an indication that you've taken risks and "got yourself together" to accomplish your goals. You are focusing your energies totally to make the risk worthwhile. If other people are involved with the situation, a Knight represents an active figure, usually male, either a mature adolescent or a young man. You are questing for something, usually knowledge or new skills. The situation may well involve schools of all kinds, as well as colleges and universities, or groups filled with energetic young people.

Pages

Pages are often representative of daughters, or young teens of either sex. A Page must learn to *serve* in order to advance, rather like being an intern in a business or political office. The Page represents a beginner, a newcomer, an apprentice, or someone taking risks to succeed. Pages indicate someone in a subordinate role—as younger people often are—learning about commitment. The Page advises challenging yourself, developing resources. You may feel hesitation or a sense of being unprepared, but you have faith the situation will turn out well. When a Page appears, it is often a promise of communication—letters, messages, phone calls, important news being delivered. You may have been waiting to hear from a college; now you will get a letter of acceptance. Some new process is causing new beginnings that need your attention in this formative period. Haste makes waste.

Tarot Play Exercise

GETTING TO KNOW THE COURT CARDS

Separate the court cards from the rest of your deck. Lay them out by rank—Kings together, Queens, Knights, Pages. Study each card carefully, noting colors and characteristics of the royal personages. Think of which cards might represent people in your life, either by astrological sign or by physical characteristics. In your Tarot notebook, list the name of each card (King of Wands, etc.), and beside the card's name list all the people you can think of that the particular card might represent in your life.

Now take another look at the court cards and see what personal qualities of your own might be represented by any or all of the cards. Choose the ones that fit and list them by name (Page of Pentacles, etc.), writing alongside the card's name the characteristics you have, want to develop, or wish you could acquire.

Interpreting the Minor Arcana

Since the Minor Arcana are not ancient symbols with deep spiritual significance like the Major Arcana, we use them primarily to glean information about real life situations and solutions. If interpreted with care and a thorough understanding of the number system on which they are based, the Minor Arcana can be very effective help for everyday problems and questions.

As you continue your study of the Minor Arcana, doing multiple practice readings and recording them in your Tarot notebook, it's also a good idea to read different books on the subject. You'll find a wide array of interpretations, not all of which agree with each other. Many experienced readers develop their own unique, free-form interpretations based on the readings they do for others and their intuitive process; others tend to use simple, basic, standard interpretations. The sources you find will overlap in an irregular way: one source will agree with another on the meaning of a particular card but disagree on the meaning of other cards. As I always stress, your *intuition* is a key factor in interpretation, and this will develop with your practice readings and continual study of Tarot, whether you use just this book or other books too.

As you progress, you will develop your own sense of the meanings of cards. Only by the time-tested method of trial and error will you discover what works best. And what works one day might not apply another time. This difference in interpretations in separate readings is the result of several things: one factor is the reader's "take" or personal philosophy (which may change over time), present state of mind, and stage of development; another factor is the *readee's* state of mind and emotions. (That's the person being read for, also called the *querent.*) Emotional factors often color a reading, especially if the other person shuffles your cards and then you lay them out. Finally, there is the factor of timing. On one day, you just might find a different interpretation than on another day. We live in a world that is always changing.

Every day, everyone on Earth is at a different level of development in the various areas of life, especially young people who are constantly learning, growing, developing, changing their minds about what they think, and moving through varying emotional states. There are countless ways of progressing through life. For example, one teenager might be first-rate at leading a group, but uncomfortable with one-on-one relationships—or vice versa. No one moves smoothly from one stage of development to another in all areas simultaneously. In this rapidly changing world, we too are constantly changing. That's what life is all about.

Always be flexible when working with the Tarot cards. Memorize the basic definitions so that you can let yourself free to flow with your intuition as you concentrate on the reading. As

INTUITION POWER

From the symbolist viewpoint, everything is interrelated, and all objects and events are connected with inner states. In theory, then, there is no action that is not at some level ritual, and all actions have correspondence on a higher plane. As magicians and occult practitioners know, all actions are significant—how you walk, sit, sleep; how you arrange your space and possessions; how and what you eat, drink, ingest. Your thoughts also have subtle vibratory powers that transverse the many levels of reality. Tarot card readings naturally draw upon this interrelatedness.

you have seen, the suits and the pips fall into general categories—once you know the basic significance, you will be able to combine these into your own interpretation, based upon a card's position in the layout. In this chapter, I present the various meanings assigned to the suits and the numbers. As you explore these meanings and test your interpretations in actual readings, you will realize that an overall system is operating.

Developing Intuition

"If a particularly important consideration comes up on which you want your intuition to work, you can concentrate on that issue, setting aside some extra time to do so. In the beginning, try not to ask too much of yourself. Be patient and keep working. Be gentle with yourself, knowing that you cannot fail because this is a natural talent we all possess.

"Be playful and avoid boredom. If your practice becomes monotonous, change the setting or practice another skill for a while. ESP does not flourish under conditions of boredom. Make up games to play. If you are concentrating on precognition, you can try guessing tonight's lottery numbers (you don't have to bet), or get a racing sheet and pick horses. It's only practice.

"How long will it take? That's up to you. Each person is an individual and results will vary. One medium I know spent five years in steady meditation before a channel opened for him. Others achieve quicker results. Much depends on your personal goals, the quality and length of time you invest, individual aptitude, and factors as yet unknown. I urge you to be patient with yourself until you reach your goal. Sometimes people work diligently for a long time and nothing seems to be happening and then, bingo!—what is called a gateway intuition occurs. It's like walking along a dull, dreary street and suddenly going through a gate into a beautiful, flower-filled courtyard hidden behind the facade of a building. This feeling is exemplified for me in *The Wizard of Oz*, when Dorothy steps out of her house into the land of the Munchkins— and the black-and-white film turns into glorious Technicolor. When you have had a gateway intuition, you'll know for sure you aren't in Kansas anymore. This is also known as the 'ah-ha!' experience, a moment of clear understanding of what before was murky."

M. J. Abadie,
Your Psychic Potential

Something of the Sun
In an apple.
Something of the Moon
In a rose.
Something of the Golden
Pleiades
In everything that grows.
　　　　　D. H. Lawrence

ELEMENTAL CORRESPONDENCES: FIRE, EARTH, WATER, AIR

Each of the four suits of the Minor Arcana correlates to one of the elements used in astrology. With some understanding of the elements, you will get a complete picture of how the different suits function from an elemental standpoint, regardless of whether you are dealing with the pips or the court cards.

Astrology considers the whole person. Inside us are varied energies that we can describe by the elements Fire, Earth, Air, and Water. These basic energies are the essential dynamic life forces. Your personal elemental makeup, which can be seen in your horoscope, shows your own individual energy pattern. Each and every person connects differently to the four energies symbolized by the elements. A water person may love to swim but hate to hike, while an earth type wants to be on the ground. And so on. The relationship of the suits to the elements gives an added dimension to your ability to make useful interpretations. It also helps to identify which people are represented by cards and to which situations they point. A grasp of these life principles and how they work is necessary for interpreting the Minor Arcana of the Tarot, and useful for self-understanding as well.

Fire: The Wands

Fire is the basic life force. Aries, Leo, and Sagittarius are its zodiacal signs. The energy of Fire is radiant. Its season is Spring (when the Sun enters the sign of Aries). Excitable and enthusiastic, Fire people are spontaneous and full of energy.

When many Wands appear in a reading, Fire energy abounds around the person, or around other people in the environment. Wands indicate much activity related to the outside world and its concerns and demands. In a teen's reading, there will be issues of work and career.

Traits of Fire Energy: Self-starting, self-confident, action initiating, decisive, outgoing, forceful, driving, active, strong, adventurous, self-expressive, self-aware, dramatic, playful, fun-loving, powerful, impressive, enthusiastic, expansive, optimistic, generous, blunt, outdoor-oriented, travel-loving, explosive, foolhardy, egotistical.

Earth: The Pentacles

The energy of Earth is in close touch with the physical plane and senses. Taurus, Virgo, and Capricorn are its zodiacal signs. Its season is Winter, the time when the Sun enters the sign of Capricorn. Known for its hard-headed practicality, Earth energy is based on the close observance of reality.

When several Pentacles appear in a reading, Earth energy is prevalent around the person or around other people in the environment. Pentacles denote issues about money and material possessions, sometimes specifying lack of sufficient funds or possessions. Security may be an issue, either financial or emotional.

Traits of Earth Energy: Organized, serious, practical, down-to-earth, realistic, ambitious, hardworking, structured, methodical, disciplined, analytical, detail-oriented, sensible, sanitary, stable, steady, reliable, productive, persistent, determined, deliberate, money-oriented, cautious, economical, self-controlled, reserved.

Air: The Swords

Air is the element of the mind. Gemini, Libra, and Aquarius are its zodiacal signs. The energy of Air is constantly shifting. Its season is Autumn, the time when the Sun enters the sign of Libra. Air doesn't like to become involved in other people's emotionally messy lives.

When many Swords appear in a reading, Air energy is strong around the person or around other people in the environment. Swords indicate mental states, obstacles, and spiritual issues. There may be strife, upsets, confusion, indetermination, unclear thinking, mental anguish.

Traits of Air Energy: Communicative, quick-witted, inquisitive, adaptable, curious, versatile, flexible, variety-seeking, relationship-oriented, cooperative, sociable, companionable, just, balanced, tolerant, impartial, intellectually detached, friendly, innovative, independent, original, individualistic, nonconformist, charming, refined, studious, babbling, nervous, superficial, mentally organized.

Water: The Cups

Water represents the intangible world. Cancer, Scorpio, and Pisces are its zodiacal signs. Its season is Summer, the time when the Sun enters the sign of Cancer. Water people are mystics and dreamers, artists, and those in touch with the deeper dimensions of life.

When several Cups appear in a reading, Water energy is active around the person or around other people in the environment. Cups point to emotions, love and romance, unconscious processes, dreams and visions.

Traits of Water Energy: Feeling, sensitive, sympathetic, nostalgic, comfort-loving, security oriented, domestic, family oriented, emotional, intense, secretive, mysterious, compassionate, benevolent, sentimental intuitive, escapist, spacey, impractical, unrealistic, artistic, inspired, receptive, moody, clinging, brooding, passive, emotionally perceptive.

Note: If the cards are reversed there may be an indication of a *lack* of the element represented.

The Court Cards as Significators

The court cards work very well as significators. Kings refer to mature males with the qualities of the various suits. In a teenager's reading, use them to represent someone in a position of authority, the querent's actual father, or a father figure. A King has wisdom and worldly experience. Reversed, you could use a King to signify a woman who exhibits the qualities of that King card.

Most readers use Queen cards almost exclusively to signify a woman who has the attributes of the suit to which the Queen belongs. Ordinarily, a Queen would represent a mature woman, a mother or a mother substitute, or an authority figure who is also nurturing and understanding. For some readings, a Queen card can signify a man with the characteristics of one of the Queens—perhaps a man deeply attuned to his own feminine nature, an artist, or an extremely sensitive man.

Knights, generally considered messengers, can signify a female as well as a male. The message will be relevant to the suit to which the Knight belongs. For example, the knight of cups might represent a girl who is bringing a message about love—or who might be about to make a declaration of deep friendship.

Page cards signify either sex. Generally, use them for a young person, an immature adult, or a child involved in the situation and related to the suit to which the Page belongs. The Pages personify messengers and messages of all sorts, coming by telephone, e-mail, and "snail mail"—any channel of communication.

TEEN TAROT TIP
Considering Gender roles

In our newly diverse society with single parents and multiple family arrangements, it is possible for a male card to apply to a female, and vice versa. For example, a woman may be playing a father role if there is no father in the family. Getting feedback from the querent is helpful when assigning a court card as a significator. When doing practice readings for yourself, consider all the gender role factors.

SIGNIFICANCE OF THE NUMBER CARDS

The pip cards of the Minor Arcana have numerological significance. Numbers are not just math used to express quantities; when looked at symbolically, each number has its own character and meaning, in both the material and the spiritual realms. Sacred numerology has a long tradition—cultures all over the world have understood the symbology of numbers and the special characteristics each represents.

With the pip cards of the Minor Arcana, the suit indicates which area of life is the focus, signifying the influences and forces about which the number is commenting. By taking both the *suit* and the *number* into consideration, you can recognize each card's applicability to the situation or question being addressed.

Ace (One)

One is the essential number for new beginnings. The Aces of the Minor Arcana are the Ones, and each Ace represents the starting point of its suit. Aces symbolize a time of seeding. Here are some key words for One: "I am," a new cycle, initiative, something new approaching, planting seeds for the future, decisiveness, self-confidence, independent action, individuality, a fresh start, new strength of purpose, new energy for an enterprise—either mental, spiritual, or material.

One is solitary. The appearance of an Ace may indicate a need to be alone or to keep everything private for the time being. Often it's necessary to go into isolation to nurture a new phase of life before going public with it.

Astrologically, One is associated with the Sun.

Two

Two is the number of duality. It refers to balance, harmony, the reconciliation of opposites. With Two, a second element or person shows up. Two serves to further what was begun at the One stage. Here are some key words for Two: "We are," choice, moderation, duality, polarity, partnerships, relationships, friendship, receptivity, joining together with not-I, union, balance, stabilization, affirmation of the new cycle, yin and yang, male and female, private and public, new opportunity.

The Two vibration is sensitive to the needs of others. It is about cooperation, waiting, diplomacy, tact, generosity to others. When Twos appear, they indicate a state of containment, either with another person or with an idea or a project.

Astrologically, Two is associated with the Moon.

Three

Three represents the universal trinity of Mind, Body, and Spirit. When Three appears, you become creative, understanding how One and Two combine to produce new births—children, ideas, creative self-expression, love. Here are some key words for Three: "We create," procreation, romance, unfoldment, recreation, happiness, celebration, optimism, entertainment, fun and games, art and writing, pleasure, travel, enthusiasm, planning, benefits of partnerships, children, completion, imagination, creativity.

Warning: Three can be volatile. Wild optimism and high self-confidence can scatter its energies. Expansion can come too fast to be contained. You may spread yourself too thin, take foolish chances, or leap before you look. Handled properly, however, Three is cheerful and fun as long as you behave responsibly and know what you are doing.

Astrologically, Three is associated with the planet Jupiter.

Four

Four represents foundations and structure. There are four elements, four directions, and four dimensions in the psychical world. Four is the fundamental number of manifestation into reality. Here are some key words for Four: that which is basic, productivity, organization, laying foundations for the future, translating plans into reality, business, financial security, earthly possessions such as real estate and property, the home and family, efficiency, challenge, working hard, stability, logic, measuring and weighing, routine, discipline.

With Four, life may be dull and dreary—all work and no play—but you have to put a firm foundation under yourself. Temporal power is indicated, often parents and other authority figures. With the Fours, you have to deal with the consequences of your actions in the real world.

Astrologically, Four is associated with the planet Uranus.

Five

Five denotes freedom and creativity, but these can challenge and disrupt the established order of Four. Crisis causes change, and change can be difficult to adjust to. Here are some key words for Five: excitement, adventure, challenge, active, physical, impulsive, dramatic, resourceful, curious, playful, a roller-coaster ride! Disruption, competition, travel, new friendships, socializing, shifts in home and family or the environment, creative solutions to problems, romantic excitement.

For those who are of a quiet and placid temperament, Five can be too much. An overabundance of excitement, new people, and new projects may make you feel you are caught in a tornado and Kansas is fast disappearing. If a matter of importance is involved, "take five" before reaching a decision or making a commitment. Slow down and get some perspective.

Astrologically, Five is associated with the planet Mercury.

Six

Six brings a new harmony after the upheaval of Five. It is the calm after the storm, bringing new equilibrium after a time of turmoil. Six is about peace and contentment, a comfortable pattern, reaping rewards. Here are some key words for Six: service and social responsibility, caring, compassion, community involvement, acceptance, domestic tranquility, family, joy, affection, love, patience, close relationships with friends, satisfaction, reconciliation, vitality, cooperation, duty, justice.

Six indicators are rarely negative. Six is geared toward service and responsibilities to others and to taking care of your own needs. The comfort that the Six vibration brings can also slip toward vegging out at home for extended periods. This is fine for a time, just don't overdo withdrawal for too long.

Astrologically, Six is associated with the planet Venus.

Seven

The essence of Seven is solitude and soul-searching. A mystical number symbolizing wisdom—there are seven heavens and seven chakras—Sevens appear when you need to delve deeply into yourself to find the meaning of what's been going on. Here are some key words for Seven: birth and rebirth, religious inclinations, the inner rather than the outer realm, retreat, sanctuary, contemplation, introspection, evaluation, study, meditation, pondering choices of the past, intellectual or occult studies, spiritual development, planning, waiting, being patient, privacy.

With Sevens showing, you may have an intense need to be alone with your thoughts and inner world. You are attracted to metaphysical subjects to help you find your true path in life. Negative cards in the reading may indicate that you are spending too much time alone and need to socialize.

Astrologically, Seven is associated with the planet Neptune.

Eight

Eight signifies abundance, prosperity, worldly goods or influence, and leadership and authority. Eight represents cosmic consciousness—the symbol for infinity is a figure eight turned on its side. Here are some key words for Eight: power, achievement, recognition, material wealth, advancement, financial gain, worldly status, acquisition of goods and property, managerial skills, financial responsibility, accomplishment, advancement, success, honor, respect, equality, awards.

Eight is a bid to develop all facets of your life—physical, mental, and spiritual. Unfavorable or reversed cards may indicate that you need to take care of your finances or you could lose money or possessions, or that you have issues around abundance or the lack of it.

Astrologically, Eight is associated with the planet Saturn.

Nine

As the final single-digit number, Nine is about endings. It indicates *integration*. You have established priorities and are ready to go on now. You are ending an old cycle before beginning a new one. Here are some key words for Nine: completion, detachment, conclusion, transition, clearing the deck, humanitarian acts and ideals, brotherhood, charity, compassion, teaching, counseling, contributions, purification, release, moving on, finishing, prioritizing, tying up loose ends, setting new goals, knowledge or higher learning, education, perfection.

Nine signifies spiritual attainment and humanitarianism. Negative or reversed cards may advise that you have lost sight of individual needs, possibly even your own, in your zeal to live up to your ideals. Don't get so wrapped up in the big picture that you neglect yourself or others.

Astrologically, Nine is associated with the planet Mars.

Ten

Ten represents both an ending and a beginning, the point of transition from the old cycle to the new cycle, which is still in process of becoming. Nine represents the completion of the cycle. As Ten can be reduced to One (1 + 0 = 1), it is about what is over and what is coming next. With Ten, it is time to let go of the old and bring in the new cycle waiting in the wings.

Periods of transition bring discomfort when you're deciding whether to stay put or move on. Although you have the option to cling to the old cycle, the Wheel of Fortune has been given another spin, and you can't just sit on the fence with a foot on either side forever, or trouble will result. *"He who hesitates is lost."* Though you can postpone the inevitable for a while, the moving finger is writing all the time—the handwriting is already on the wall; it's best to heed what it tells you.

Though it is a form of One, Ten has more impact. With Ten it's like climbing a spiral staircase—you can look down and see where you have been from a higher level of awareness. Tens challenge you to make the choice of whether to stagnate in what's familiar and comfortable, a rut, or to embrace the new cycle whole-heartedly and start something new. Now's the time to challenge yourself and develop to a higher level.

As there are only nine planets, Ten does not have a planetary correspondence. Instead, it is associated with the Wheel of Fortune.

Quick Numerology Reference

One = New beginnings. A new cycle.

Two = Duality. Union. Relationships.

Three = Self-expression. Communication.

Four = Foundations. Hard work.

Five = Creativity. Freedom.

Six = Duty. Service. Others' needs.

Seven = Solitude. Seeking. Higher education.

Eight = Abundance. Power. Prosperity.

Nine = Endings. Completion. Humanity.

Ten = A new cycle coming into being.

Tarot Play Exercise

GETTING TO KNOW THE NUMBER CARDS

Separate the forty Minor Arcana number cards out of your deck and spread them out so you can see them all at once. Study them for a while. Contemplate how each makes you feel. Then fill out the following play exercise.

Date: _____

Cards I was drawn to:

Cards I found especially appealing:

Cards I found disturbing or unappealing:

Key points for appealing and unappealing cards:

Note a preference for one or more suits of cards:

Describe reasons for preference:

Separate the cards into sets of numbers and find a key word for each set of number cards:

Aces: _____

Twos: _____

Threes: _____

Fours: _____

Fives: _____

Sixes: _____

Sevens: _____

Eights: _____

Nines: _____

Tens: _____

Note: If necessary, use additional sheets of paper for writing down your feelings about the number cards and put them in your Tarot notebook.

The Wands

In medieval times, Wands were representatives of those who worked on the land and did manual labor. The "working classes" possessed little and were usually attached to great noble houses. Thus, over time, Wands have acquired a general meaning of being related to the work one does or plans to do.

Although they are specifically related to work activities, Wands are less materialistic than Pentacles and are concerned with the areas of work involving innovation, entrepreneurial enterprises, and the communications aspects of business and commerce.

Related to the element Fire, the appearance of Wands suggests self-starters who are leaders and can motivate others through relationships and creativity.

KING of WANDS

KING OF WANDS

As Wands relate to business and enterprise, the King of Wands exemplifies the leader, entrepreneur, promoter, and public figure. These types may be found in many areas of employment—the media, advertising, politics, communications, entertainment— whatever puts them in the public eye. The King of Wands points out a personality that radiates warmth and vitality, both physical and mental. Freedom is important, but he can be quite forceful in getting his own way. Often he owns his own business and travels constantly.

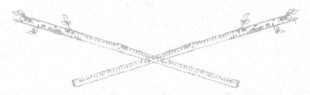

Upright

This King represents an influential and independent person, usually a man, who is in a position to help you (or the querent) and is favorable toward you. He may be your father, a boss or a mentor, a teacher or professor, or an advisor. Honesty, intelligence, and fair-mindedness are his qualities, and he gives good advice. He is a loyal friend worth cultivating. If there is not an actual person in your life with whom you can identify him, he refers to a situation where "what you see is what you get." There's no danger of deception or hidden agendas. His appearance suggests good fortune coming your way—unexpected assistance or counsel, good news, an increase in status, an unexpected honor or award for good work.

KEY WORDS FOR THE KING OF WANDS UPRIGHT
Someone in charge. Loves a challenge. Enthusiastic. Enterprising. Motivated. Ambitious. Helpful. Full of passion. Mature. Fatherly. Strong. Intelligent. Successful. Influential. Decisive. Independent. Active. Optimistic. Generous. Creative. Unexpected income. An inheritance.

Reversed

The King of Wands reversed suggests snarls, unexpected complications, or delays in any project you are starting. Someone whose help you need either won't be available or will refuse to help. If he represents your father, you may be at loggerheads with him over the issue and not have his moral support. If the card doesn't identify a real person, you will have to work extra hard for success in your enterprise. Reversed, the card may be telling you to develop your own King of Wands type qualities so that you will get what you are after. The situation is favorable, but you may not get the help you want. Still, you can make it come out right if you try hard enough and have faith in your abilities.

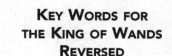

KEY WORDS FOR THE KING OF WANDS REVERSED

Delays. Hypocrisy. Suspicion. Arrogance. Non-cooperation. "My way or the highway." Bossy. Intolerant. Devious. Unyielding. Close-minded. Overbearing. Dogmatic. Opinionated. Stubborn. Controlling. Biased.

QUEEN OF WANDS

This Queen is regal, warm, dignified, strong, independent, and pleasure-loving. A dynamic figure, she is affectionate and proud of her children, getting involved in their extracurricular projects. However, she likes the spotlight and can be so busy with her own interests that she has little time for her children. Her personal style is active and busy. She may have a job with many responsibilities or be involved in community activities. With a lot of flair and charisma, she is popular for her energy, capability, and self-assurance.

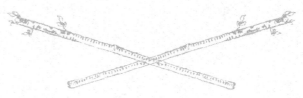

Upright

The Queen of Wands may represent your mother or a mature woman such as a teacher or older relative who is inclined to help you out with projects and give you good advice and counsel. She has a knack for bringing together the right people to make things happen. She is lively and creates an interesting environment. She asserts her independence and makes no bones about her sexuality. Creative herself, she recognizes talent in others and does what she can to promote it. If this card doesn't fit a person in your life, it points to this being a propitious time for you to move forward in any creative project or enterprise you are planning. In a teen's reading, she reports that you have her qualities within yourself and challenges you to develop them.

KEY WORDS FOR THE QUEEN OF WANDS UPRIGHT

Career-minded. Loves life. Active. Popular. Sexual. Social. Affectionate. Inspired. Creative. Demonstrative. Business acumen. Energetic. Versatile. Passionate. Involved with children. Warm-hearted. Home-loving. Generous. Enterprising. Innovative. A positive thinker. Encouraging. Giving.

Reversed

When reversed, this Queen can represent a woman with power over you who wants to control you and your activities as payment for her advice and assistance. She may control the purse strings in the family. Her strong ego needs demand attention and she likes to manipulate social situations for her own advantage and glory. When she does give her help, her motives may actually be self-serving rather than generous. If the Queen isn't indicative of a person you can identify, when reversed this card is a warning to be alert and avoid offending a woman who is in a socially powerful or other important position that may affect your life and your advancement. There may be deception, greed, and jealousy.

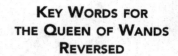

KEY WORDS FOR THE QUEEN OF WANDS REVERSED

Shallow. Self-serving.
Narrow-minded. Seeks control.
Demanding. Deceptive.
Neurotic. Ruthlessly ambitious.
Untrustworthy. Dominating.
Jealous. Manipulative.
Envious. Strict. Egotism.
Emotional blackmail.

KNIGHT OF WANDS

This Knight represents the energy of Fire—ready for action on a rearing charger. Highly self-reliant, this Knight indicates someone who gets what they want by being excited about their ideas and taking positive action. Very enterprising, he or she pursues their interests avidly, gathering all materials necessary for a project and being enthusiastic about its successful outcome. Action is the key here—whether in sports or other competitive activities. If this is you, you go after what you want with energy and enthusiasm and achieve your goals. Resourcefulness and love of freedom are also qualities of this Knight, who isn't concerned about other people's opinions and often fails to get permission for adventures.

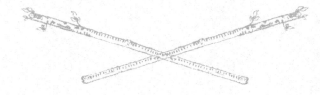

KEY WORDS FOR THE KNIGHT OF WANDS UPRIGHT

News of an important event. New friends. Restlessness. Change. Travel. Athletic competitions or activities. Generosity. Impetuousness. Visitors from afar. New experiences. Adventure. Good news. Humor. Optimism. Excitement. Movement. Sexual exploration. Relocation. Departures.

Upright

Knights are messengers. When the Knight of Wands appears, expect good news about work or social matters. The glad tidings can be about any happy event to which you are looking forward—a vacation or trip, acceptance into the college of your choice, a school event such as a prom date, an engagement or marriage. If a specific person is represented, he or she will share the qualities of the King and Queen of Wands, the parents in the royal family. Thus, the person bringing the message is trustworthy and loyal.

Reversed

Reversed Wands aren't ordinarily negative, but the reversed Knight means a delay in receiving an expected message or communication. If you are waiting for money or an invitation to a social event, you don't get it when expected. Delay regarding an important communication results in your getting frustrated and impatient. A planned trip may be called off due to weather conditions or airline difficulties. Your or someone else's engagement or wedding may be postponed or canceled. Reversed, this Knight points to separation.

Page of Wands

The Page of Wands usually faces sideways, holding a tall staff with both hands, in an attitude suggesting forward action and vitality. Often holding a staff with leaves growing out of it, this Page signifies growth and may denote a child or childlike qualities.

As the Fire page, he embodies positive qualities of artistic talent and flair, imagination and creativity. He can also be impulsive and unpredictable. This Page brings new ideas and suggests adventures to come. He indicates the start of a new phase in your creative development. You may receive a message about this from a new person in your life who is inspirational or artistic. Or, you may embark on some new creative project of your own or be offered the opportunity to study for a creative career.

Upright

The Page of Wands represents an enthusiastic youth, eager to express the outgoing, active qualities of Fire. Inquisitive and excitable, this person is alert, interested, and bright, but may lack concentration or scatter energies all around. This Page brings communications—phone calls, letters, e-mail—and it's usually pleasant news. It can mean a special announcement of importance to the questioner, or an especially busy time in your life, filled with communications flowing back and forth. If the Page doesn't represent a person, the situation is one in which you are dealing with new things, ideas, people, environments. Romance may be in the air—maybe you are on the phone or e-mailing a new love interest.

Key Words for the Page of Wands Upright

Messages. Communication. Good news. Important tidings. Information. Children and adolescents with Fire qualities. Self-promotion. Enthusiasm. Quick responses. Extroverted. Sexually intrigued or aroused. New ideas. In the limelight. An interesting event. New learning. Romance. Friends.

Reversed

The reversed Page of Wands means troublesome delay. Something or someone will not arrive on time, due to mischance or irresponsibility. A message may be unwelcome news that disrupts the routine of your life. It could be a "Dear John" letter. Or someone has betrayed your secrets. You may have to travel to set things right. If representative of a person, it is someone bringing false or misleading news or information, someone not to be trusted.

ACE OF WANDS

Upright

The Ace of Wands means the beginning of new growth, physical or material, high energy, and a position of strength. It promises new things to come, usually having to do with enterprise—school, extracurricular activities, sports, work, the public. When the Ace of Wands appears, you are full of energy and strongly motivated in a new direction that will implement your overall growth. You have lots of vitality for whatever you want to undertake. This is a launching time for whatever is new—ideas, technologies, adventure, friendships, career plans, travel to foreign countries. Your health improves.

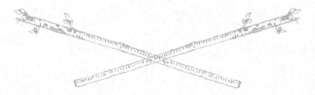

Reversed

The Ace of Wands reversed indicates blocks to your progress and growth. You may be stuck in the old cycle, struggling to enter the new one or refusing to move on to new things. You need to "let go and let God." You lack energy, a result of overdoing it or a stressful lifestyle. You need more rest and exercise to combat sluggishness and fatigue. Your health is under par, or your energies are being sapped by circumstances.

KEY WORDS FOR THE ACE OF WANDS UPRIGHT

Ready to go. Eager to start something new. A new phase of your life. High energy. High expectations. Optimism. Self-confidence. Strong abilities. A turning point. Setting forces in motion for future growth and advancement. Exciting opportunities.

KEYWORDS TO THE ACE OF WANDS REVERSED

Lack of money. Funds not materializing. Delays in getting funds. What's promised doesn't come. False starts. Futile efforts. Lack of imagination. Cancellations. Waiting, waiting, waiting. Feeling powerless. Uninspired. Unambitious. Unproductive. Lack of enthusiasm for beginning anew.

Two of Wands

Upright

The Two of Wands shows that a second element is entering into the situation. There is an element of surprise. Choice is called for; you may have to choose between equally desirable things, persons, or situations—colleges, romantic interests, invitations, athletic activities, music instruments, projects, jobs, or living accommodations. Your energies are divided, maybe between school and work, between your parents, or between different groups of friends. You have seeded something at the Ace and are now "waiting for your ship to come in."

Reversed

Reversed, the Two of Wands emphasizes the surprise factor, and it could be a nasty one. You may have made the wrong choice and are regretting it. Your forward movement is being impeded by circumstances or people, causing frustration. Cooperation is proving difficult for you. You have a problem with friction due to inequality of power or status in a relationship. Ego is getting in the way of progress. You need more time to make a decision, to think things through, get advice, back off, and recoup.

Key Words for the Two of Wands Upright

Opportunity. Early stage of a project. Off to a fine start. Partnership. Collaboration. Cooperation. Joint ventures. "The world is your oyster." Moving forward. Travel or receiving visitors from abroad. Achievement of goals. Looking forward. Anticipation. Hope.

Key Words for the Two of Wands Reversed

A waiting period is irksome. Loss of interest in the enterprise. Delays. Lack of cooperation. Self-doubt. A relationship gone sour. Disagreements with others. Nothing happening. False expectations. Unfulfilled hopes. Disappointments. Lack of energy. Failed enterprise. Misfirings.

THREE OF WANDS

Upright

Usually concerned with business and commerce, in a teen's reading the Three of Wands can imply that you are learning about business, preparing for a business career, thinking of getting an M.B.A. or a degree in telecommunications in anticipation of working in the field of communications. This card suggests you are broadening your interests to include more of the world beyond your immediate environment, looking outward to see what's there for you in terms of a career and reward for your efforts. You might become an exchange student and go abroad to further your studies, or find some other opportunity to learn while traveling.

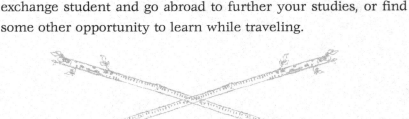

Reversed

You are working on an internal level to clarify your purposes and firm up your sense of self-direction. The time is not yet ripe to go public with your ideas for new projects. You may need to ask for help but are too proud to do so. Opportunities have slipped away from lack of action, or you have failed to seek them out. You may be suffering creative blocks or hesitating to get your thoughts and ideas out there.

Four of Wands

Upright

An extremely positive card, the Four of Wands suggests the formalization of social status and relationships. It can mark a coming-of-age celebration such as a bar or bat mitzvah, graduation from any level of school, awards presentation ceremonies, engagements, marriages, or other occasions marked by special rituals. Focus is on the home life. Your family may be buying a new house, adding amenities to the present one, or planning a family reunion party. This card also points to your self-identity, the foundation of your life, and how you envision your future. This is a time for serious goal setting, moving to a new level of your development, looking at career options, making plans for your future.

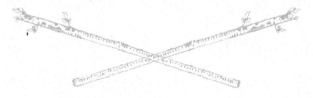

Reversed

As this is such a positive card, the reversed position merely softens the effect: you are having a quiet celebration at home rather than a noisy public one. Success is less public, but still sweet. You are resting after a period of hard work. A relationship is noncommittal.

KEY WORDS FOR THE FOUR OF WANDS UPRIGHT

A special celebration to mark a new stage of development. Joyful times. Achievement commemorated. An important event. Happy home life. Laying firm foundations for the future. Prosperity. Semester break. Coming of age. Hard labor's reward. Relaxation. Holidays or vacations. Romance.

KEY WORDS FOR THE FOUR OF WANDS REVERSED

Identity problems. Lack of self-esteem. Failure to manage challenges. Lack of a solid foundation. Self-expression thwarted. Lack of personal space at home. Celebrations or ceremonies delayed or postponed. Some sort of a breakup. Insecurity. Lack of support.

KEY WORDS FOR THE FIVE OF WANDS UPRIGHT

External obstacles or conflict. Rivals. Need for vigor and action. Standing up for yourself. Holding the line. Competition. Physical activities. Sowing wild oats. Rebelling. Hanging out with the guys. Seeking challenges. Assertiveness. Overcoming obstacles positively.

KEY WORDS FOR THE FIVE OF WANDS REVERSED

Squabbling over trifles. Struggling with obstacles. Losing a competition or opting out. Sports or athletic activities unsatisfactory. Internal conflict or difficulty making a choice. Bickering with siblings or friends. Travel plans gone awry. Inability to take a stand.

Upright

Conditions are changing rapidly, bring in new ideas and experience. You are looking for variety and excitement, wanting to break out of an old stagnant situation. Ordinary routines have become stultifying, and you are eager to go in search of new action, new situations, new people. You may be involved in a competition—scholastic, athletic, popularity, and so on. The challenge is great and it requires all your energy and strength to meet. Conflict may be a problem; egos may be clashing. Adrenalin is running high. Group activities are predominant, and the influence of peers, crowds, or audiences can be a factor, possibly stressful. There is much stimulation in the environment. You seek novelty, different experiences.

Reversed

Reversed, the Five of Wands indicates a need to challenge yourself to make the changes you desire. You can't be passive now; if you are, nothing will change. You're bored, but not up to the effort that change takes. Combativeness puts you off. Danger can come from association with gangs or mobs. You might get in trouble or be hurt by deciding to go along with the crowd against your better judgment. Unexpressed resentments may be troubling you.

Six of Wands

Upright

You are in equilibrium now, having overcome forces that were opposing you. Your identity feels secure. You're in your groove. You're at a stage in your development where you feel content with who you are. You've resolved self-doubt through accomplishment. Having faced some challenges and won, you are ready for the next step forward. You have proved to yourself that you can handle what comes your way, take responsibility, and not lose perspective. Social and scholastic success is at hand. You are riding high in triumph, victorious and feeling good about yourself. At ease with your crowd, you shine socially and people find you likeable. Everything and everyone works together smoothly with no conflicts.

KEY WORDS FOR THE SIX OF WANDS UPRIGHT

Victory. Awards. Accomplishment. Acclaim. Conquest. Achievement. Rewards. A triumphal march. Public recognition. Winning. Having "the right stuff." Encouragement from others. A scholarship or an academic honor. Goals fulfilled. Problems solved. Battles won.

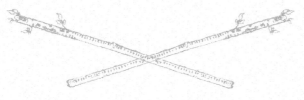

Reversed

You are suffering a disappointment. Something you worked hard for didn't pan out, or someone blocked your efforts. Your self-confidence is low but your potential is still great. You are unsure about your goals or how to accomplish them. You may be shy of performing in the limelight or being highly visible. Public appearances may give you stage fright and anxiety. You just need more practice and experience to get the success you want.

KEY WORDS FOR THE SIX OF WANDS REVERSED

Losses or losers. Dreams that didn't come true. Failure. Loss of hope. Feeling insecure or insignificant. Needing reassurance. Being "second banana." Not up to the challenge. Shyness or insecurity gets in your way. Lack of communication. Misunderstandings. Disappointment. Betrayal.

SEVEN OF WANDS

Upright

When the Seven of Wands appears, it means you need to take a stand, to fight off obstacles and opposition. You are able to meet the challenge, but you must have your defenses in good order. You are being tested—your beliefs (political, religious, social) are being called into question and you have to defend them or change them. Your plans for your future—career or lifestyle—may not be getting the approval you want. Creative projects dear to your heart aren't being recognized, possibly because you are going against conventional thinking. Being yourself is on the line. This is a battle for survival. It may be a long, lonely one. Take heart—you will win in the end because of your energy and endurance.

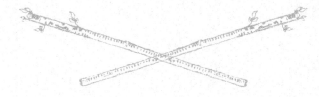

Reversed

You are being given a hard time for what you believe or how you dress, behave, or think. Some kids are called derogatory names, such as "geek," "nerd," "freak," or "weird," if they are artistic or unconventional. Cheer up! These are the very people who go on to make huge contributions to our society. Think Bill Gates. You are feeling like an outcast but you aren't alone. Stick to your guns. Don't allow yourself to be intimidated.

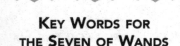

KEY WORDS FOR THE SEVEN OF WANDS UPRIGHT

Fighting the good fight. Standing up for what's right. Being the embattled loner. Forging an identity. Being unfashionable or unconventional. Going it alone. Holding firm against all opposition. Standing your ground. Strong beliefs. Strength of character. Individual pride. Artistic and creative endeavors.

KEY WORDS FOR THE SEVEN OF WANDS REVERSED

Criticism. Lack of approval or understanding. Feeling like an outcast. Being different. Fighting uneven odds. Retreat from confrontation. Withdrawal into one's self. Being shamed. Reluctance to face problems. Vulnerability. Lack of self-assertion. Fear of rejection.

EIGHT OF WANDS

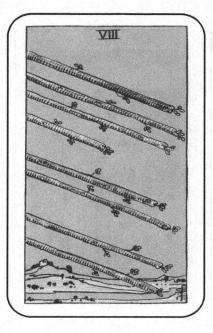

Upright

Happy landings! You've shot your arrows into the air and they are landing where you wanted them to land. Everything is A-okay and all systems are go. You've come through a period of stagnation and are now in rapid forward motion. Your energies are focused, you've tied up the loose ends, completed your projects, and are on the brink of a new phase of life. Maybe you are graduating from high school and about to enter college or the work force. Or you've brought a really big and important project to a successful conclusion and are ready to move on to something even bigger. A plane trip may be in the cards, perhaps to visit a college or interview for a job. Whatever is in process is likely to succeed.

Reversed

You may be upset by a move or a trip you can't avoid. Or the fast pace of events has you frazzled and overwhelmed. You may be scattering your energy to the four winds, rushing about with no place to go. Delays are frustrating. Plans, especially for travel, are postponed or canceled. Forcing issues now is not a good idea. Keep cool and go with the flow.

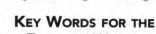

KEY WORDS FOR THE EIGHT OF WANDS UPRIGHT

Rapid movement of events. Quick results. Activity. Movement. Action. Readiness. Mind-expanding experiences. "Full steam ahead." The ball is rolling. Making headway swiftly. Getting there. A sudden romance. Travel by air. Creative inspiration. Good news. Welcome communications.

KEY WORDS FOR THE EIGHT OF WANDS REVERSED

Premature movement. Excess haste. Wasted energy. Going nowhere fast. Impulsiveness. Ill-considered action. Bad news. The arrows of jealousy. Scattered efforts. Things all up in the air. Not getting where you want to go. Changes of plans, delays. Quarrels or disagreements. Backing up.

Upright

You've done the job and done it right. Your discipline and abilities have carried the day. You're now in the power position with the obstacles behind you. You've chosen a path, and it is working. Now you can move to a higher level of development—in school, in athletics, in relationships. You have achieved sufficient independence to be able to stand on your own two feet and feel secure there. There's more work to be done, but you have strength in reserve. You've shown courage under fire and are able to defend your legitimate territory. Moving forward with a sense of purpose and direction, you are able to take on multiple tasks because of your increased effectiveness. You can protect yourself if need be.

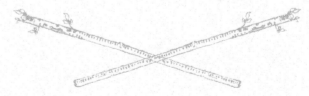

Reversed

You are being distracted from your goals. Your strength is waning because of improper use. Problems have developed because you are displaying more strength than necessary—stubbornness, obstinacy, lack of cooperation.

KEY WORDS FOR THE NINE OF WANDS UPRIGHT

Standing guard. Your right to self-defense. Hanging on to gains. Knowing your rights. Self-protection. Perseverance. Being king of the hill. Good health and a strong constitution. Taking care of your body. Physicality. A step away from final victory. Courage and determination. Recovery. You need to get better at self-advocacy, handling your own needs, and looking out for your own interests. Challenges seem too great for you.

KEY WORDS FOR THE NINE OF WANDS REVERSED

Defenseless. Defensive. Off guard. Unaware of dangers. Nonconfrontative. Out of your league. Unassertive. Won't take a stand. Need more preparation. Feeling inadequate. Refusing to compromise. Not being alert. Being dependent. Fear of fighting back. Lack of conviction.

TEN OF WANDS

Upright

You are taking up new responsibilities as a result of a new situation. You may feel burdened down, but your strength and character will carry you through anything, even an extremely difficult task. Teens especially can be asked to carry extra responsibilities if there's a crisis in the family. Or higher levels of education bring added, sometimes heavy, burdens. You may be handling a large project virtually without help, but the end is in sight, and you will cope with everything as you go along. Extra work may have been voluntary, or necessary if you're to get ahead. Either way, you took it on willingly. And it may soon be lifted. This card often indicates the born workaholic.

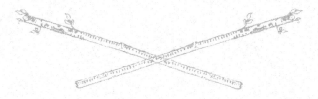

Reversed

You may be carrying burdens that don't belong to you. It's as if the whole world is on your shoulders. You could be "carrying" someone who isn't pulling their own weight, maybe even a parent. If you're shouldering a heavy load and need help, ask for it. Although you're strong, you're overtaxing yourself and it could make you ill. If there's a family crisis causing your load, consult with responsible adults outside the family.

KEY WORDS FOR THE TEN OF WANDS UPRIGHT

Heavy responsibilities. Taking on a big load. Working extremely hard. Meeting all commitments. A highly demanding project or course of study. Feeling overloaded. No time for yourself. Handling things efficiently. A drive toward success no matter how difficult. Being in the final stretch.

KEY WORDS FOR THE TEN OF WANDS REVERSED

Oppression. Overburdened. Unfair responsibilities. Too many projects or activities. Being worn out. Weariness. Musculoskeletal difficulties. Faltering strength. Resentment. Striving toward unreachable goals. Expecting too much of yourself. Being unwilling to ask for help.

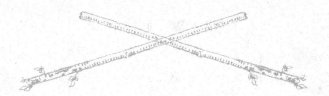

Tarot Play Exercise

GETTING TO KNOW THE WANDS

This is an easy and fun exercise that will test your knowledge of the Minor Arcana pip cards and give you some practice in relating the number cards to their meanings.

First, separate the pip cards (Ace through Ten) in your deck into the four suits. For this exercise, choose the suit of Wands. Arrange them in numerical order, from Ace to Ten. Next, without referring to the meanings just given, examine your cards and see what you remember about each number's meanings. Use the illustrations on your particular deck to help you fix the meanings in your memory. (That's primarily why the pip cards are illustrated in most decks—as an aid to memory.)

Now, in your Tarot notebook under "Wands," list the numbers Ace through Ten and jot down whatever key words and phrases you remember, or any spontaneous ideas that pop up. After you've done this, go back and check your list against the meanings given in this chapter for the Wands pip cards.

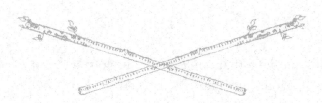

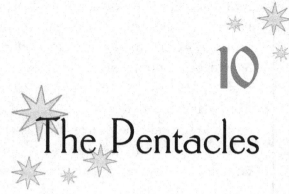

10

The Pentacles

The Pentacle is a symbol in magick (spelled with a *k* to differentiate between the serious practice and the kind of stage-show, rabbit-out-of-the-hat kind of entertainment commonly called *magic*). The Pentacle is considered to have great power to protect against harmful influences. Thus, in this most practical of the suits, a deeper meaning implies that money can be used for higher purposes like philanthropy. Also, money and material wealth aren't necessarily without a spiritual component. For example, if you own a piece of real estate and you place it in a trust for preservation of open land, that is a way of preserving the environment.

So, if you have any negative feelings about money, remind yourself that as long as you earn it, spend it, and handle it honorably—for the highest good of all concerned—money is beneficial.

Therefore, Pentacles strike a positive note on a temporal theme. Pentacles are related to the element Earth, indicating groundedness in the physical world. And since most people have to work to earn a living, they point to whatever is or will be your livelihood.

WEALTH AND SPIRITUALITY

Money has often gotten a bad rap from those who want to follow a spiritual path. We've all heard the saying, "Money is the root of all evil," but this is actually a misquotation. The original saying is, "The love of money is the root of all evil." Often, through misunderstanding and observing the misuse of money, we feel that money itself is somehow intrinsically bad, and that having or wanting it isn't spiritually worthy. That is not the case. *Poverty* causes most of the problems in the world, and its eradication will solve many of them. When wealth is both gained and used with a spiritual perspective, rather than from greed or only for profit, it takes on a positive cast.

KING OF PENTACLES

As Pentacles relate to money and material goods, the King of Pentacles represents those who flourish in our money-based economy—CEOs, bankers, stock traders, lawyers, professionals, technocrats, entrepreneurs, business owners, and so on. Thus, this King exemplifies those who understand money, how it works, and the power it confers. He also portrays those who desire to upgrade themselves financially. In a teen's reading, he may be a corporate executive with whom you are interviewing for a job, or a banker from whom you are soliciting a loan.

Upright

This king represents a mature man of subtance. He is also a courageous man, a solid citizen, reputable and concerned with the welfare of others. A symbol of worldly power in a positive sense, he is firmly established in his own right and experienced in money matters. His stability makes him able to provide reliable advice about money and finance. As he is inclined to be helpful to younger people, he suggests a person who is a patron of the arts and sciences through venture capitalism and therefore someone who is cultured and refined. He enjoys being a sponsor or a mentor. If he is not an actual person, his appearance implies that you are either engaged in some worldly enterprise or planning a successful one.

Reversed

Some think this King reversed is extremely negative, representing actual physical danger, but in my view what it represents is the negative side of money and business practices—greed, dishonesty, shady dealings, overconcern with earning power, use of money as a weapon, controlling through holding the purse strings, lack of business acumen, crudeness or rudeness, thinking that money makes the man, using wealth as the sole measurement of a person's worth, believing that the end justifies the means, one who constantly worries about money or is tightfisted with it. The man represented by the card in a teen's reading may well be your father, who may be lacking in the fatherly qualities you desire.

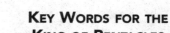

KEY WORDS FOR THE KING OF PENTACLES REVERSED

Materialistic. Domineering. Greedy. Money is all that matters. Fraudulent. Unreliable. Stingy. "Everyone has a price." Mean. Lack of refinement. Boorish. Male chauvinist pig. Suspicious. Workaholic. Absent father. Opinionated or bigoted. Rigid. Bad manager of money. Insensitive.

QUEEN OF PENTACLES

This Queen is a fascinating combination of the Earth Mother and the practical businesswoman. She knows how to handle money and she likes cultivating the Earth. Often she has her own investment portfolio, which she watches carefully. Or she may be devoted to the management of her home, where she has a myriad of projects going on. Skilled at tending to others' needs, she is a good mother and has superb organizational ability. She makes things run smoothly at home and at work. Her children have physical comforts, but she may not show her affection or emotion.

KEY WORDS FOR THE QUEEN OF PENTACLES UPRIGHT

Good mother, cook, household manager. Nurturer. Nature lover. Hospitable. Good business acumen. Handles money well. Resourceful. Prosperous. Kind. Confident. A green thumb. Efficient. Organized. Emotionally mature. A businesswoman. Patron of the arts. Maternal. Down to earth. Helpful.

Upright

The Queen of Pentacles is a competent and mature woman and a concerned parent. Often old-fashioned in her outlook, she tries to make sure her kids understand the practical realities so necessary to life—she'll teach them how to cook, do laundry, shop, balance a checkbook. She enjoys working with her hands and welcomes a gracious lifestyle supported by abundant resources. If not a person in your life, this card predicts material gain, financial increase or security, and perhaps interest in the domestic side of life. You may be setting out on your own, getting an apartment, preparing to manage your own life and finances, working and earning money. You may be receiving financial assistance from a woman.

Reversed

When reversed, this Queen can be a cold and distant mother who does little for her children's welfare, or is extremely demanding and rigid. Overly concerned with outwardly appearances, she may be unhappy with her financial situation. Her fiscal irresponsibility may cause problems with debt or lack of abundance. She can be petty and ungenerous both with funds and spirit. A pretentious attitude can make her insufferable. Her values are skewed toward materialism as the greatest good. She may suffer from self-doubt, greed, lack of confidence, sexual frustration. If not a person, this card can represent an unstable situation where there is financial insecurity, fear of poverty, or emotional deprivation.

KEY WORDS FOR THE QUEEN OF PENTACLES REVERSED

Overworking. Socially conforming. Narrow-minded. Self-important. Unable to show affection. Emotionally cold. Distant. Hypercritical. Workaholic. Lacking nurturing qualities. Financially reckless. Overspending. Picky about details. Worrier. "Keeping up with the Joneses."

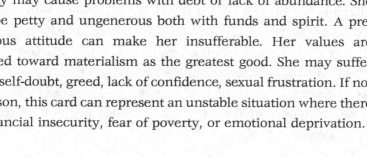

KNIGHT OF PENTACLES

This Knight represents the energy of Earth—cautious, capable, competent, resourceful. Grounded in material values, he is even-tempered and reliable, emotionally steady and full of common sense. In no rush (he is usually seen on a standing rather than a charging horse), he takes his time to weigh options before making decisions. He brings a message about money, usually good news, or about a departure or an arrival. Although he has the spirit of adventure, he is materially-minded. Good at executing any job or work required, he is, however, unlikely to be a self-starter. His appearance may predict some other changes in your life relative to your money.

KEY WORDS FOR THE KNIGHT OF PENTACLES UPRIGHT

Important material concerns. New developments. More money. Good news regarding income. Attention to detail. Careful planning. Conservative attitude. Dependability. Patience. Common sense. New adventures in the natural world. Animal lover. A faithful lover.

Upright

The Knight of Pentacles represents someone who is diligent, responsible (especially with money and property), conscientious, and willing to do whatever is necessary to get the job done. He may indicate that you are getting involved in a new project, some earth-type task such as building or environmental clean-up. If romance is the question, this card is a person you can trust to be serious and committed. However, the relationship will develop slowly and be primarily physical in nature. Another meaning is movement—travel or a move planned well beforehand.

Reversed

The Knight of Pentacles can foretell an unwelcome message—about money, a loss, a disappointment, expectations gone wrong, frustration, unforeseen delay, a job or college application turned down because of botched paperwork. Your previous plans may have to be altered. You might expect obstacles to the development of a love relationship or an unwanted move or change of residence. If a person, the card may be a youth who is unemployed or uninterested in employment. If not a person, the situation may involve money problems, and these may be causing depression, inertia, and low motivation.

KEY WORDS FOR THE KNIGHT OF PENTACLES REVERSED

Loss. Disappointment. Money problems. Financial instability. Being underpaid or cheated. Poor judgment about finances. Wastefulness. Lack of planning skills. Depression. Apathy. Feeling stuck. No inspiration or energy. Your get-up-and-go got up and went. Refusal to take any risks.

PAGE OF PENTACLES

The Page of Pentacles is known as the card of the student or scholar. It represents a youth intent on his studies, ignoring what is going on around him. He is usually shown standing in an outdoor setting, holding a Pentacle before him as if studying or admiring it. This suggests the desire for money, or learning how to make it, usually through education.

As the Earth page, he is stable and reliable, carrying ideas of unfolding material capabilities. The new beginning may be vague, but it contains great potential for the development of skills and talents that will bring material rewards. You may come under the influence of a practical person who encourages you to attend to such qualities in yourself.

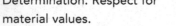

KEY WORDS FOR THE PAGE OF PENTACLES UPRIGHT

Quiet. Reflective. Realistic about goals. Practical. Diligent. Serious-minded. A bookworm. An introvert. A good friend. A student. A nature-lover. Written messages, often about money. Educational opportunities. Slow but steady progress. Determination. Respect for material values.

Upright

The Page of Pentacles represents a studious youth with the qualities of Earth—ambitious, determined, goal-oriented, intelligent, sensitive to Nature and the arts, and appreciative of the good life. This Page may signal that you are becoming aware of your body in new ways, perhaps to improve your health. You are learning constantly, possibly in a work-study program. If your question concerns a relationship, he is a warning to let things take their natural course and not rush into anything prematurely, especially sex. If this Page does not represent a person, he points to your worldly ambitions and communications about them; you may be getting e-mail, letters, phone calls, or doing paperwork.

Reversed

The reversed Page indicates the opposite of the upright position. A young person refuses to study or hates or skips school. Lazy, lackadaisical, unwilling to put forth the effort to learn, this person is uninterested in education and achieving goals. If not a person, it means bad news about money or disappointment such as failure in an exam or failure to gain admission to the college of choice. Serious effort and proper focus are lacking.

KEY WORDS FOR THE PAGE OF PENTACLES REVERSED

Rebellious. Unmotivated. A troubled teen or child. Learning disabilities. Moody youngsters. Superficial knowledge. Money problems. Unexpected expenses. Bad or disappointing news. Lacking common sense. Extravagance. Boredom. Inactivity. Not interested in learning. Insufficient education.

New beginnings concerning money or income. New enterprise will succeed. Tangible results on the way. Health improvement. Body work. Early stages of a project. Students getting their diploma or degree. Bodily pleasure. A salary increase. New opportunities. Monetary aid.

KEY WORDS TO THE ACE OF PENTACLES REVERSED

Delays with money matters. A money-making idea fizzled. Broken promises. Stinginess. Poor fiscal management. Lack of knowledge about money. Misuse of funds. Haste makes waste. Receiving less than you expected. Dashed hopes for financial improvement. Fatigue. Poor health. Hard to get going.

Upright

The primary card of new success, new money, and new enterprise, the Ace of Pentacles is extremely positive, predicting money coming your way and success of new projects or investments. You are working toward new goals whose aim is your financial betterment. You are planting the seeds for your future financial security. The Ace strongly indicates prosperity coming toward you. You could receive a gift of money, a scholarship, financial aid for college. Or you could be going on a major shopping trip to prepare yourself for your future earning capacity.

Reversed

When reversed, this Ace indicates you are having trouble focusing on your schoolwork, projects, aims, and goals. Success is delayed or difficult. You may be in poor health or lack energy for the necessary work. Things will pan out eventually, if you are patient and avoid getting discouraged to the point where you quit or give up on yourself. Work on being more grounded and centered to achieve prosperity.

Two of Pentacles

Upright

There are two possibilities for the Two of Pentacles: either money coming from two sources, or having to make a choice between two different options. If a relationship is involved, you may have to choose between two loves. Or it may be that you have the choice of two colleges, two jobs, or two extracurricular activities. You are adapting to circumstances. The message is: make a choice and stick with it, whatever the outcome.

Reversed

Money is tight. You may be holding down more than one job to cover expenses, or juggling what money you do have to make ends meet. You may be juggling not only sources of income but options for change. If a relationship is involved, perhaps you and your lover are being pulled in two different directions. Hang tight for the time being until you get clear on what's best. Use affirmations to overcome doubt and worry.

THREE OF PENTACLES

KEY WORDS FOR THE THREE OF PENTACLES UPRIGHT

Skills learned well. Accomplishment. First job. Getting noticed. Work with status. Talents recognized. Competence. Opportunity to demonstrate skills. Good grades in school. Certification or graduation. Off to a good start. Getting paid for creative work. New social status.

KEY WORDS FOR THE THREE OF PENTACLES REVERSED

Poor performance. Lack of skill, confidence, or ambition. Lazy or uninterested. A half-hearted effort. Fear of failure. Insufficient training. Bad grades or failing to graduate. Lack of purposeful direction. Oversensitive to criticism. Missed opportunities. A goof-off.

Upright

Usually connected with a skill in a profession or trade, this card indicates you are now able to turn this skill to profit, and gain success. You might be a recent graduate or soon to be a graduate. If you are inclined toward art or a craft, this card betokens inspiration and success. The motto, "Do what you love and money will follow," applies. You are enterprising and therefore can expect to earn good money from your craft. Traditionally, this card predicts work to come. Teens may find an opportunity to display their creative abilities in a local fair, show, or community project. In turn, this could lead to opportunities for commissions or employment as you prepare for action in the "real" world.

Reversed

Either you need more training and practice or you aren't making the effort to acquire the skills you need for your chosen work. Your concern about succeeding and making money may be holding you back from trying to get employment. Fear of failure may be a problem, or lack of competence or self-confidence. You must gain more trust in your abilities and be willing to take a risk now. Attitude is as important as your basic skills.

FOUR OF PENTACLES

Upright

The Four of Pentacles suggests you are holding tight to whatever money and material possessions you have. Because you are basing your important life decisions on security issues, you are unable to take risks that might improve your situation. This conservative attitude is good if you are trying to avoid immature behavior, but it may be a hindrance when you need to try new things and experiences. If you feel threatened about financial security or the stability of your home life, you are trying to prepare yourself by closely guarding what you have. You or those around you are fixated on the status quo and fearful of change. Over time, you will overcome your fears and build a secure financial base.

Reversed

You are hanging on to your possessions or a life situation—possibly a romance—for fear of changing anything. Or you may be in a comfortable rut or a state of inertia. However, change is necessary, and you have to accept that it will come whether you agree or not. You may be trying to make something happen prematurely, or be quarreling with someone over money or material goods you feel you need, such as a car, clothing, or equipment. Perhaps you have squandered your money unwisely and regret it.

KEY WORDS FOR THE FOUR OF PENTACLES UPRIGHT

Holding on to what you have. Slow but solid learning. Financial security. Home life. Managing money conservatively. Passing a school exam. Learning economics. Being careful with funds. A secure base. Acquisition of material goods. Balancing your budget. Living within your means.

KEY WORDS FOR THE FOUR OF PENTACLES REVERSED

Hanging tight. Unwilling to let go. Threatened by change. Financially insecure. Fear of lack. Failure to pass an exam. Bad at managing money. Not getting what you need or want. Fixated on material things. Lack of privacy at home. Quarrels over money. Loss of a job or other resources.

FIVE OF PENTACLES

Upright

Most writers give this card a basic negative message of poverty, financial losses, and material lack. However, the number Five suggests adventure, creativity, dramatic excitement, and the enjoyment of worldly pleasures. If there is lack, spiritual bankruptcy is probably the root of the unfavorable condition. This Five warns that money may soon be very tight, or that support—such as a grant or stipend—won't be coming. Some change in material conditions is likely. Stress and worry over finances can cause illness. There may be a disruption in home life—a move, a divorce (causing financial hardship), or a deliberate choice to live frugally without many material goods to advance a spiritual cause.

Reversed

You are advised to get your house in order, both financially and spiritually. It's time to cut your losses and move on as best you can to avoid further deterioration of the situation. Avoid going into debt or taking financial risks. Antisocial behavior should be curbed. Teens may be affected financially by their parents' actions or be forced to contribute to family support by getting a job.

KEY WORDS FOR THE FIVE OF PENTACLES UPRIGHT

Lack of faith or spiritual principle. Material want. Unemployment. Feeling abandoned. Loss of what you counted on. Change in financial or social status. Going it alone. Health problems. Realizing money can't buy happiness. Compassion for others less well off. Charity. Neediness.

KEY WORDS FOR THE FIVE OF PENTACLES REVERSED

Unheeded warnings cause poverty. Spiritual awareness comes into focus. End of hard times. Unconventional lifestyle. Dealing with the poor. Helping others. At loose ends. Emotional neediness. Relationships based on materialistic values. Unavoidable risk. Fear of making changes.

Six of Pentacles

Upright

With this Six, financial problems are over and abundance, prosperity, and personal gratification are available. Students will get the financial assistance they need, parents' income may increase dramatically. There is or will be plenty to "share and spare." You are inclined to be charitable because you are in a balanced position regarding income and outgo. By using your prosperity to help others, you create material good coming to you and good going out from you. This card predicts life getting back to normal—or improving—through cooperation with others. Relationships will be creative partnerships, harmonious and equal, not based on emotional or financial neediness. Social life is pleasant now.

Reversed

You need to watch your spending. Don't be extravagant and go into debt. You may not be able to help others as you'd like. Demands are being made on your finances. Your social life is less active, and you can't spend much on entertainment. Others are being non-cooperative. In relationships, you need to work to create harmony and understanding, especially about your differing mutual attitudes to money and spending. One person may be thrifty while the other is a spendthrift, and this can cause arguments and dissension. You are recovering from a period of loss and confusion. Now is a good time to find a workable lifestyle that will give you security and peace of mind. This will require effort from all concerned.

KEY WORDS FOR THE SIX OF PENTACLES UPRIGHT

Getting your "just deserts." Being charitable. Enough to share and to spare. Overcoming financial problems. Payment of debts. Cooperation with others. Gifts given and received. Money's no problem. Financial assistance. Using your talents to help others. Grants. Loans. Awards.

KEY WORDS FOR THE SIX OF PENTACLES REVERSED

Bad luck with money. Mismanagement. Lack of sufficient funds. Getting over a bad period. Debt. Selfishness. Disagreements about money and how to spend it. Loss through carelessness. Gifts with strings attached. Being too demanding about material things. Uncharitable. Uncooperative.

Upright

Seven is about the ability to imagine the future—in this case, your future career or work, how you will earn money. It's about making your dreams come true in the concrete world of material reality. Along with imagining your future, you have to actually lay the groundwork by preparing yourself for it in terms of the course of study you pursue, doing your homework, getting the grades for college entrance, or learning the skills for the practice of a trade. It's a card that says, "When the going gets tough, the tough get going—and *stay* going." It's about perseverance and about wise planning for the future. What you need now are clear goals, a realistic purpose, and determination to stay the course no matter what.

Reversed

The Seven of Pentacles reversed often shows up when teens can't imagine a particular future for themselves. This can be due to social pressure to conform to family values, especially for girls who are discouraged from advanced studies or who unwisely marry early and quit school to have a family. Some feel that certain occupations are simply closed to them because of their background, ethnicity, or education. They may lack role models for what they want to be; but this difficulty can be overcome by creative visualization of goals. Fear of failure can also be a problem, especially with those not fully supported by their families. But in the end, it is really all up to you.

EIGHT OF PENTACLES

Upright

This card suggests learning a new skill or preparing for a career by training intensively with a clear goal in mind. You are integrating previously learned skills into a new form, or acquiring new skills. Sureness of purpose predicts success and quite possibly financial gain at a new venture, a new job, or a new project. You are now figuring out how to use your resources, both mental and physical, to fulfill your needs and allow for expansion. You may be apprenticing at a craft. If so, craftsmanship will be rewarded by commissions and new business. You should keep a professional attitude when looking for a job or presenting yourself for new training.

Reversed

When this card is reversed, it indicates that you have not finished your studies, or have not mastered the necessary skills to achieve your goals or ambitions. You wish to begin some new enterprise, but you lack sufficient knowledge or haven't yet clearly defined your goals. Or you are unwilling to put in the extra work to attain the skills you need. Possibly you are in bad health, lack vitality, or get bored too easily. You need "stick-to-it-iveness" to overcome the obstacles in your path. Getting a second wind after long, sustained effort will help you along.

KEY WORDS FOR THE EIGHT OF PENTACLES UPRIGHT

Apprenticeship. Education. Further skill training. Gaining experience. Job search. Work-study programs. Use of natural talents. Productivity. Self-employment. Computer skills. A hobby that earns money. Enterprise. Doing the job right. Taking courses and reading books about a subject.

KEY WORDS FOR THE EIGHT OF PENTACLES REVERSED

Frustration. Hard work fails to pay off. Poor health. Lack of vitality. Sick of responsibilities. Disorganization. Bad study habits. Getting it together is difficult. Impatience. Inattention to details. Haste makes waste. Unrealistic about goals. Expecting instant gratification.

Upright

The Nine of Pentacles suggests self-reliance and independence from financial concerns and worries, usually a result of your own efforts and temperament. You have a strong desire to be your own person and to make your own way in the world. You are quite mature for your age. As a personality, you are strong and sure of yourself; you have learned self-discipline and are resourceful. You know how to allocate your resources and work hard on self-improvement. You are focused on solid accomplishment, not trivial pursuits. Quite possibly you are an earth sign. You listen to the counsel of adults you respect, and benefit from it. You are setting yourself up to enjoy a plentiful future without money worries.

Reversed

You are dependent upon someone else for financial security, probably your parents or other relatives. Independence eludes you, or it will take some time to achieve. You are living modestly because you have no choice. Your goals may be fuzzy, preventing you from earning what you want. You may lack family support, or your family may be of modest means. If a romance is involved, you may be avoiding commitment, secretly preferring the single life. Dependency may be irksome, but you are stuck with it until you can make it on your own. Getting real with yourself will help.

KEY WORDS FOR THE NINE OF PENTACLES UPRIGHT

Material abundance. Good future planning. Financial security. Prosperity. Independence. Good advice. A mature personality. Realistic goals. Desire to achieve. Wealth oriented. Determined to succeed. Standing alone. Self-mastery. Solitude. Ownership. Property, real estate. Self-sufficiency.

KEY WORDS FOR THE NINE OF PENTACLES REVERSED

Shaky finances. Dependency. Poor decision-making ability. "Money doesn't matter." Lack of privacy. No time to yourself. Money hassles. Frustration over restrictions on your freedom. No social life. Trying to break free. Death of a loved pet. Can't get focused. Life is difficult.

Ten of Pentacles

Upright

This card says "family" and indicates several generations of a happy one, with property and money inherited. It's that which is solid and reliable, such as land and good investments. You may be entering a family business, or inheriting money to start your own some day. Or you are ambitious to start a family and create wealth yourself. You may be drawn to a career that pays well, such as corporate management, the law, or financial institutions. If romance is involved, you are looking for someone with a similar background and compatible heritage. You want a successful, well-connected, landed family life. You want to think big, bigger, biggest, in order to achieve social prominence and prosperity.

Reversed

This card indicates a troubled or dysfunctional family who isn't able to support your needs and goals. You may lack sufficient funds for your education because your family can't or won't provide the money. Your parents and other family members may be constantly quarreling and upset over finances. Often, a focus on financial problems within a family can have a negative effect on teenage children, who don't feel the security they want and deserve. You may be flaunting family traditions to show your independence, causing flare-ups constantly.

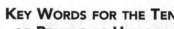

KEY WORDS FOR THE TEN OF PENTACLES UPRIGHT

Family connections. Legacies. Inherited wealth. Trust funds. Old money. Financial security. A happy home life. Several generations together. Transfer of properties. A dynasty. Parental support and assistance. Marriage into a wealthy family. Major life transitions.

KEY WORDS FOR THE TEN OF PENTACLES REVERSED

Family quarrels, usually over money or inheritances. Financial losses or problems. Lack of family support. A disputed legacy. An ill parent or family member. Discord in the family. Feeling burdened by family needs or demands. Sibling rivalry. Family disapproval of engagement or marriage.

Tarot Play Exercise

GETTING TO KNOW THE PENTACLES

Here is another round of the exercise you did at the end of the last chapter. It is a fun and easy activity to test your knowledge of the pip cards and give you some practice relating the numbers to their meanings.

As before, separate the pip cards (Ace through Ten) into the four suits. For this round, choose the suit of Pentacles. Arrange them in numerical order, from Ace to Ten. Next, without referring to the meanings given in this chapter, examine your cards and see what you remember about each number's meanings. Use the illustrations on your deck to help you fix the meanings in your memory. (Remember, that's primarily why the pip cards are illustrated in most decks—as an aid to memory.)

Now, in your Tarot notebook, list the numbers Ace through Ten under "Pentacles." Jot down whatever key words and phrases you remember, or any spontaneous ideas that pop up. After you're done, go back and check your list against the meanings given for the Pentacles pip cards.

The Swords

Some people consider the Swords totally negative, but there is a spiritual element connected to the Swords. Although Swords can represent extremely difficult events, obstacles, conditions, or states of mind, often we embark on a spiritual path as a result of intense suffering—physical, mental, psychological, or emotional. Remember the saying, "Life is pain. Pain makes you think. Thinking makes you wise. And wisdom makes life endurable." Mentally oriented, Swords are associated with the element Air, which represents mental activity. Swords by their nature are sharp and cutting—but this isn't all bad. They can cut through foggy thinking and leave you clear-minded.

KING OF SWORDS

The King of Swords is shown as a serious, sometimes stern-looking man, with drawn sword ready for action as he reflects on options and possibilities. He is a lover of knowledge and of law and order. His chief quality is his use of his mind to attain emotional detachment and enable him to make long-term plans and decisions based on analytical thought and logic. Thus, the King of Swords is emblematic of a spiritual path undertaken mentally, as a development of the conscious mind.

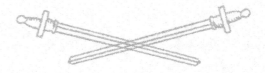

Upright

This King represents great strength and authority. His appearance involves your mental processes. As a person, he is someone involved with mentally demanding work, such as a professor, a researcher, a lawyer, or a military officer. A good counselor with acute mental dexterity, he thinks clearly and rapidly, expressing his thoughts articulately. He might be your father or another authority figure who is a good advisor. As a teenager, you may be occupied with questions concerning your life values, thinking about and revising your old belief system, or attempting to define your true philosophy of life. When he appears, you may be on the verge of a spiritual breakthrough about which you are ready to communicate. He can also represent a spiritual inner guide figure.

KEY WORDS FOR THE KING OF SWORDS UPRIGHT

Rational. Cool. Fair. In command. In control. Unprejudiced. Ambitious. Self-assertive. Analytical. Unemotional. Ethical. Expert. Spiritual aspirations or achievement. A man concerned with your welfare. An intelligent professional. Advisor. Authority figure. Law and order. Mental work. Strong character.

Reversed

Reversed, this King exemplifies the negative qualities of the Air signs—someone who is over-rational, distant, unapproachable. If he represents your father or another authority figure, he may be impossible to understand or get close to. He is demanding, especially intellectually, and insists that you toe the line he lays down. He can be an absent father or one who has a hard time communicating with his children. If not a person, he represents a situation that forces you to confront an authority that is antagonistic to your own personal beliefs or your desire for a spiritual life; this could be a specific church or peer group. You are advised to keep these matters to yourself and not reveal them to unsympathetic people.

KEY WORDS FOR THE KING OF SWORDS REVERSED

Domineering. Demanding. Anti-spiritual. Hard-headed. Fickle. A bad communicator. Unfair treatment. Someone using words as rapiers to wound. Malicious gossip. Superficial friend. Playing one against the other. Fixed opinions. Injustice. Intimidation. Violence. Aggressiveness.

QUEEN OF SWORDS

As the female counterpart of the King, she represents the emotional side of the mental processes. She is a formidable figure of power and authority, either in the mental world or in the spiritual realm. Her domain includes emotional loss and bereavement. If she fits your mother, you may have lost that parent to death or divorce, illness or desertion. Or perhaps your mother is excessively demanding and unable to show affection. However, she is not all bad, as she usually has her children's welfare uppermost in her mind; but she lacks softness and is a harsh disciplinarian.

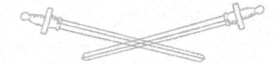

Upright

When the Queen of Swords appears in a teen's reading, it's a sign of loss and separation, such as a divorce or widowhood. If she represents a real person, she tends to approach child rearing as a scientific project, reading all the latest books, programming strict schedules, and insisting on homework perfectly executed. Quite probably, she is a professional woman. She is strong-willed, with the strength to cope with loss and get on with her life. If she does not represent a person, you may be going through an emotionally devastating experience that is related to a severe loss.

Reversed

Reversed, this Queen represents someone not dealing well with sorrow or loss. Sadness, withdrawal, mourning beyond reasonable limits are affecting her ability to function. If she fits your mother or another female relative, the woman may be depressed and neglecting her children. She may be angry and unreachable, which makes you feel alone and left out. If not a person, she may indicate a situation where you are bogged down emotionally, wallowing in your pain, blaming an unkind Fate for your troubles. If a relationship is in question, there may be power struggles. Conversely, she can advise that you are neglecting your spiritual development to the detriment of your overall growth and may need help.

Knight of Swords

KNIGHT of SWORDS .

This Knight is usually portrayed as a young man rushing ahead, his battle sword drawn upright. As such, he represents someone who is ready and willing to demonstrate intellectual prowess, skill, and power through sharp intellectual competition. He suggests someone who is eager for mental challenges and seeks them out just to prove the ability to win. Young adults today are especially challenged mentally in our new information age and must develop computer and other high-tech skills to make their way when they enter the world of work. This card can indicate that you are not using your energies to the best advantage—perhaps scattering them to the four winds in your eagerness to show what you can do.

Key words for the Knight of Swords Upright

Sudden change. Many comings and goings. Messages flying back and forth. An unexpected turn of events. Intellectual conflict. Impulsive action. Taking a chance. Assertiveness. Boldness. Mental excitement. Going full speed ahead. Single-mindedness. A platonic relationship. Resoluteness.

Upright

The Knight of Swords may bring news of conflict, not usually physical but mental, such as serious differences of opinion around you, causing angry messages to be sent and received. You may be involved in an intellectual competition, such as a debate or other school-oriented contest. You may be thinking of joining the military as a means of achieving a higher education. Or you may be so focused on your intellectual pursuits that you are neglecting other areas of your life. If a relationship is involved, it may be primarily one of mental stimulation and good talk.

Reversed

When reversed, this Knight becomes passive and does not take the required action. This is a bad time to initiate new projects. You are delaying doing something that is necessary, for example, getting your theme paper written or your college applications filled in and mailed. You may be avoiding getting down to hard study and procrastinating about your responsibilities. This could have serious repercussions. If it represents a person, this card would mean someone who brings unwelcome news or an untrustworthy person prone to hasty acts and rash decisions. It could be you yourself.

Someone in opposition. A sudden departure. An unwelcome arrival. Excessive haste. Impatience. Deceit. Action without thought. Premature action. An aggressive youth. Bad company. Belligerence. Use of force. Quarrels over ideas. Sarcastic or wounding words. A significant man leaves suddenly.

PAGE OF SWORDS

The Page of Swords is about taking mental risks. You may be experimenting with some new line of thought and communicating with others about it, possibly over the Internet. You are learning to be intellectually oriented—especially if you're in your mid to late teens—by exploring abstract concepts and focusing on intellectual ideas. This Page may represent a younger sibling or other child whom you are helping to develop mental capacity. Or it signals your experiments with different courses of study to see what holds your interest and suits your career plans. Communication is an important part of this process, and you are learning communication skills that will serve you well, as long as you use them seriously.

KEY WORDS FOR THE PAGE OF SWORDS UPRIGHT

Unexpected or unsettling news. Adjustment to unwanted changes. Sharp communications. Criticism. Mental tasks. Important information arrives. Need for rational thought. Delayed action. Unfinished business. A significant document. Dealing with sensitive issues. A conflict.

Upright

This Page can relate to you or to a younger person, depending on your age. He may bring news of problems or difficulties regarding a young person. You or someone you know may be behaving in a risky manner. Motivated by a desire for unconventional activity, the person represented can cause strife in the family or at school. If the card does not represent a person, there is a situation going on involving many communications. For young people, this could be with teachers or other authority figures regarding grades or conduct. If the Page is you, it may mean that you are the deliverer of bad news.

Reversed

When reversed, the person represented by this Page is having a hard time getting it together. This young person may be appealing and charming, but he or she isn't to be trusted. If the card represents you, you may be trying to pull the wool over somebody's eyes, or be sponging off your parents or friends. The reversed Page is associated with spying. You may be scoping out something that's none of your business; or someone else may be trying to get at your secrets. If a younger person, it's a brat who is being sneaky or is capable of spiteful action. Be on your guard.

KEY WORDS FOR THE PAGE OF SWORDS REVERSED

Spying. Trickery. Bad news. Malice. Sneakiness. Spitefulness. Gossiping. A malicious tongue. Being watched. Keeping secrets. Nosy kids. Hypocrisy. Intrusiveness. Deceit. Misunderstandings. Backbiting. A two-faced friend. A rumor monger. An aggressive child. An unpredictable youth. Ill health.

ACE OF SWORDS

Upright

Like all of the Aces, this Ace indicates a new beginning brought about by a triumph over difficulties, in this case by mental means. It is symbolic of a major breakthrough and suggestive of a brand new lifestyle ahead. You have earned this opportunity by using your mental faculties at a high level. There may be conflict, but you have the strength of will to cut through obstacles now. You may have to stand up for your ideas and beliefs because you feel under attack. If you avoid making enemies, you will succeed in any new enterprise because you are very focused.

Reversed

As this Ace is always a positive card, the reversed position merely suggests delays in plans or projects, or unexpected glitches gumming up the works temporarily. Your mental preparations and efforts may be stymied and not coming into physical manifestation as quickly as you had hoped, which is causing you frustration and tension. You may undergo minor surgery or hurt yourself with a sharp instrument. Take care!

KEY WORDS FOR THE ACE OF SWORDS UPRIGHT

Problem solving. The cutting edge. Intellectual power. Getting it together. Freedom to go your way. Strength in adversity. A strong sense of self. New spiritual growth. Standing up for your beliefs. Good results of struggle. Right on the mark. Right action. Rational thinking.

KEY WORDS FOR THE ACE OF SWORDS REVERSED

Bad timing. Unexpected delays. Plans postponed. Frustration. Idleness. Minor surgery. Sharp objects or words. Opposition. Obstacles. Illness. Muddy thinking. Scattered energies. Injustice. Self-mutilation. Legal difficulties. Insensitivity. Coming on too strong. Cutting out.

Two of Swords

Upright

This card represents a situation in which you feel it is impossible to move forward. You are stuck—simply maintaining a state of balance by denying the tension underneath. However uncomfortable you feel, you aren't yet ready to make any changes. Eventually, however, change must occur, or the tension will become unbearable. You need to *communicate* about the problem and stop pretending that things are just fine. You may be called upon to show tolerance of another's beliefs. You do have options; remove the blindfold and look squarely and honestly at the situation.

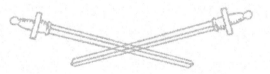

Reversed

When the Two of Swords appears reversed, the action starts to flow again after a period of blockage and frustration. You feel freed to move and get on with it. Communication revives because the source of disagreement is gone or compromise is agreed upon. If a romance is involved, you are now able to reach reconciliation. You are out of the area of conflict or have decided to walk away from the dispute.

KEY WORDS FOR THE TWO OF SWORDS UPRIGHT

Blocked. Stalemated. At a crossroads. In denial. A tense situation. Keeping it all inside. Refusing to look at what is. Deadlock. Waiting. Unable to decide. Suspension. Suppressed emotions. Keeping the lid on. No action. Feeling overwhelmed. Unable to make a fresh start. Passive.

KEY WORDS FOR THE TWO OF SWORDS REVERSED

A sigh of relief. End of stalemate. The decision is made. Movement is back. Action is taken. Tension relieved. Release. Feelings are aired. Lines of communication are cleared. Emotions come to the surface. Reconciliation with loved ones. Getting along with others.

THREE OF SWORDS

KEY WORDS FOR THE THREE OF SWORDS UPRIGHT

Heartache. Separation. Sorrow. Being hurt. Mourning a loss. Crying your eyes out. Lost love. Inner turbulence. Your heart is bleeding. You've been stabbed. "Love's labor's lost." Inconsolable sadness. You feel your pain. Letting go of the past. Tension. Upheaval.

Upright

The Three of Swords is a card of severance. It tells of separation and sorrow, often the end of a romantic relationship. However, the final result is positive. The separation or breakup was necessary: the relationship had outworn its value, or you outgrew it. Even though you feel sorrow or regret, it has happened for the best, and you'll soon realize this truth. Right now, feeling the pain intensely, it's hard to believe you'll get over it. Don't try to hold on to the past. Let it go. It must be allowed to disintegrate within your psychic structure.

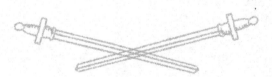

KEY WORDS FOR THE THREE OF SWORDS REVERSED

Stressed out. Getting over it. Getting help for depression. Sorrowing. A love triangle. Denial. Troublesome third parties. Repressed emotions. Rejection in love. Unrequited love. Recovery from loss and suffering. Health problems. Minor surgery. Handling sharp instruments.

Reversed

Instead of looking the facts in the face, you are looking for someone to blame for the separation or loss. You need to start thinking clearly about the truth of the situation. You can't see your own part in the breakup and are in a state of self-pity, falling into depression over what's gone but not forgotten. Own up to your faults and learn from your mistakes. Don't get bogged down with the "what-might-have-beens."

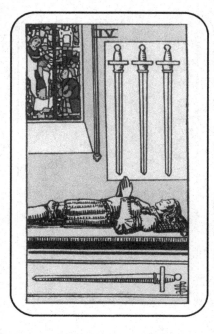

Four of Swords

Upright

A card of rest and rejuvenation, the Four of Swords indicates recovery from what ailed you: emotional or physical stress or illness. You are at a point of working on your problems quietly, and you need a period of solitude and introspection to get perspective on recent experiences. You have been in pain but now are taking the first steps to recovery. This card represents the calm after the storm, a time of being away from other people, of claiming your own space again to get your inner house in order. You need to be able to say no to excess demands on your time.

Reversed

You are not permitting yourself the rest and solitude you need after a period of turmoil. You may make yourself ill if you refuse to get rest. Everyone requires calm and quiet to recover fully from a disruption of regular life. You are no exception. Stop trying to be a hero. Look out for your health. Take time out. Go on holiday, or keep to your room. Learn to set boundaries. Get in tune with the need for self-protection.

KEY WORDS FOR THE FOUR OF SWORDS UPRIGHT

Time out. Rest and recuperation. Peace. Stability. Being enclosed. Calmness. Silence. Solitude. Self-defense. Setting boundaries. Claiming personal space. Protection. Regeneration. Cutting back on activities. Slowing down. Regrouping. Taking a vacation. Introspection. Recovery.

KEY WORDS FOR THE FOUR OF SWORDS REVERSED

Refusal to rest. Break time is over. Getting back into action. Overdoing. Giving in to others' demands. Relinquishing personal space. Ill health. Action postponed. Family tensions. Inability to open up with others. No safe space. Slow starts. Stress increase. Unpleasant activities.

FIVE OF SWORDS

Upright

You are adjusting to change resulting from distress or loss. An abrupt event has required a painful adjustment. New challenges lie ahead and you have to be ready to meet them. The past is over and best forgotten. If someone or something disappointed you, you were expecting too much. Change is an uncomfortable process but a necessary one. Whatever is being changed—your lifestyle, your location, your beliefs, your self-image, your friends, your relationships—it is for the best. This card shows the double edge of the sword. One side is defeat, misfortune, betrayal, and loss; the other is accepting the inevitable boundaries life presents. You or someone you know may be attracted to conflict and underhanded ways of dealing.

Reversed

Reversed, this card warns of unpredictable or untrustworthy people whose motivations are hidden, or there is a situation that is complex and hard to fathom. You may be trying to extricate yourself from a bad crowd and fear repercussions. You've been badly burned and have taken it hard; now you need a period to recoup. Your trust in others has been shaken, but you have to hang on and be more careful in the future where you place trust.

Six of Swords

Upright

You are moving away from troubles, putting the past behind you. This card proclaims the beginning of a new phase after a time of upheaval, a new period of smooth sailing with relatively few problems. Your situation is stabilized, which gives you a new peace of mind. Harmony and decreased tension prevail. After intense suffering, you are back in sync with yourself or with another person, and feeling good about yourself. This is a time of integration, or reintegration. New friends, romance, and opportunities come into your life, and you can trust their stability. This card also suggests a journey over water, or relocation to another place to live. Luck is on your side, and any change you make will have a good outcome.

KEY WORDS FOR THE SIX OF SWORDS UPRIGHT

Goodbye troubles. A new phase of life. Good times ahead. Blue skies. Moving away (sometimes literally) from pain and suffering. A happy transition. Leaving it all behind. Getting on with your life. Being together. Going with the flow. Travel over water. Relocation. Calmness.

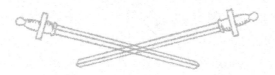

Reversed

This card reversed implies difficulty in finding solutions to vexing problems. Rough waters are keeping you off balance, emotionally or physically. You may feel there is nothing you can do to alter the situation, what with the lack of cooperation you feel with others; but improved skills in communication will help. You could be in a difficult transition time—between junior high and high school, or after a move, or romantically.

KEY WORDS FOR THE SIX OF SWORDS REVERSED

Rough sailing. Negative thinking. Fighting the current. Paddling upstream. Expected relief delayed. Frustration with progress. Slow going. Stuck in a rut. Can't get out of an old pattern. Cancellation or postponement of a trip. Obsessing over past problems. Lack of action.

Upright

This is a self-contradictory card, with elements of inventiveness and risk-taking, and also of deceit and underhandedness. For teens, it could mean fierce competition in school or on the athletic field, friends who aren't what they seem, or rivals who don't play fair. Roundabout action or indirect communications clog up the works. You can't take people and promises at face value. You have to rely on your wits to handle the situation, and you have to use your wit to achieve your aims. Overconfidence could do you in. You need prudence and caution to get the upper hand in a tricky situation.

KEY WORDS FOR THE SEVEN OF SWORDS UPRIGHT

Things aren't what they seem. What you see isn't what you get. Caution. Trickery. Duplicity. A close call. Escaping by guile. Putting one over. Evasiveness. Winning by chicanery. Craftiness. Indirect action. Unfair competition. Self-defeating attitudes. You are your own worst enemy.

KEY WORDS FOR THE SEVEN OF SWORDS REVERSED

Clowning around. Underhanded behavior gets caught. Getting your own back. Stolen goods returned. Just deserts. Mental flexibility wins the day. Redistribution of goods. Turning to others for advice and counsel. Taking care of practical concerns. Getting your act together. True friendship.

Reversed

When reversed, you need to keep mentally flexible to respond rapidly to challenges and changes. You have to keep a sharp eye out for unexpected turns in a situation. You may be trying out new ways of thinking, or experimenting with different lifestyles in a secretive manner. Going it alone to prove your individuality may prove difficult. Isolation or lack of understanding is a problem. Learn to express yourself openly.

EIGHT OF SWORDS

Upright

When this card turns up, you feel trapped—either unable or unwilling to make a choice or change a situation that is keeping you in a painful state of mind. Meanings include being caught in a bind, not feeling permitted to be yourself, inability to act independently, feeling tied down by circumstances you can't control. Although many writers view this card as extremely negative, it can represent your ability to focus totally on your aims and goals. Also, you are not without resources to change matters. The bad situation is temporary.

Reversed

This card reversed alleviates some of the problems. You have recognized the need for change and are starting to free yourself from restrictions. Progress is coming, if slowly. Negotiations, possibly with your parents, have eased the restrictions. You have more freedom of movement and are more able to express yourself openly. Someone incarcerated is released. Your awareness is increasing, especially about human rights.

KEY WORDS FOR THE EIGHT OF SWORDS UPRIGHT

Restrictions. Feeling trapped. All tied up. Can't get loose. Grounded. Isolated. Boxed in. A vicious circle. Inhibitions. Lack of energy. Confusion. Depression. Being a victim of circumstances. Lack of confidence. Unable to go forward. Fearful. Stuck.

KEY WORDS FOR THE EIGHT OF SWORDS REVERSED

Freedom. Release from restrictions. A new attitude. Removal of obstacles. Reconciliation. A fresh start. Making amends. No more fear. Empowerment. Out of the pressure cooker. Understanding the problem. Overcoming prior restraints. Conquering fear. Seeing your way clear.

Anxiety. Nightmares. Negative thinking. Fear. Grief. Worry. Obsessing over past misfortune or pain. Thoughts going round and round your brain. Unable to rest. Depression. Insomnia. Feeling inadequate to cope with the situation. Needing professional advice. Unable to handle emotions.

Upright

The Nine of Swords is called "the nightmare card," and it depicts someone who has been unable to sleep peacefully due to anxiety, tension, unhappiness, or regrets over past errors or misfortunes. You are in an unhappy and troubled mental state, even if the facts don't warrant such painful thoughts. Your mind is tortured by extremely negative thinking—"worst case scenario" stories or horror fantasies. You may actually be having nightmares caused by deep-rooted factors trying to surface for recognition and resolution. If you are deeply troubled, please get some psychological counseling or speak to a trusted adult.

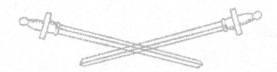

A ray of hope. Sunnier times. Good news. Our worst worries seldom come true. Free of stress and worry. Feeling good about yourself again. The storm is over. A light at the end of the tunnel. Peaceful sleep. A new day is dawning. Faith in the Universe.

Reversed

Mental torture is forcing you to change. The crisis situation you are suffering is because you fully grasp the cause of your problems. Resolute honesty will give you the insight to improve your situation. Crisis circumstances, no matter how painful, are not all bad. Nine is the number of completion. Thus, this Nine predicts that the necessary changes you are being asked to make promise a better future.

TEN OF SWORDS

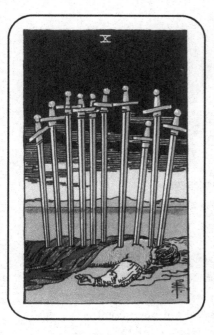

Upright

Although it's a grim card, this Ten predicts the end of your present trials and tribulations and the beginning of a new cycle. It says that you have to clear away what remains of the old cycle. Even though it might be extremely painful, you'll make a clean break from past pain and suffering, leaving no loose ends. For teens especially, this card shows that life goes in cycles—alternating between difficult and easy. Problems always come about and have to be solved. Attitude is all. You make your own reality by what you think.

KEY WORDS FOR THE TEN OF SWORDS UPRIGHT

Gaining maturity. Letting go of the past. Learning from your mistakes. Ending a cycle. Family conflicts. The death of old ways. Finding a new belief system. Recurring problems need solving. Everything has an ending. Necessary changes. It's darkest just before the dawn.

Reversed

When the Ten of Swords appears reversed, you are resisting taking the necessary action to move yourself forward into the new cycle. However, delay tactics or kidding yourself about the truth won't stop the change from coming. Change is inevitable. It's how you grow and develop. The sun must rise on each new day, and if you make excuses for yourself or someone else to hang onto the status quo, you will only prolong the agony. Do something; make a move, even if it's the wrong one.

KEY WORDS FOR THE TEN OF SWORDS REVERSED

A step in the right direction. A change for the better. Being ready for new challenges. Getting yourself together. The worst is over. Pain is a great teacher. Surviving. Help from others. Solving problems. Getting on with your life.

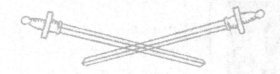

Tarot Play Exercise

GETTING TO KNOW THE SWORDS

Here's the third round of the exercise to test your knowledge of the pip cards while giving you some practice relating the number cards to their meanings.

Separate the pip cards into the four suits. Of course, this time you'll choose the suit of Swords. Arrange them in numerical order, from Ace to Ten. Next, without referring to the meanings given in this chapter, examine the cards and see what you remember about each number's meanings. Use the illustrations on your deck to help you fix the meanings in your memory. (Again, that's primarily why the pip cards are so often illustrated—as an aid to memory.)

Now, in your Tarot notebook, list the numbers Ace through Ten under "Swords," and jot down whatever key words and phrases you remember, or any spontaneous ideas that pop up. After you've done this, go back and check your list against the meanings given for the Swords pip cards.

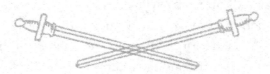

12
The Cups

The Suit of Cups is a happy one, representing love, harmony, affection, friendship, and compassion. Cups are rarely negative and can offset any difficult cards in a reading, often pointing to a way out of a difficult situation. Cups also suggest creativity—artistic or musical ability—or creative solutions to problems. As the Cups are related to water, they indicate feelings and emotions rather than mental activity or concern with the material world. Cups also point to the spiritual realm. Because they are containers, Cups symbolize receptivity and their images are usually beautiful, evoking ideas of nurturing and fulfillment. They hint at moods and the changeability of their element, Water. Cups can also be indicators of unconscious processes of which we need to become more aware.

KING OF CUPS

The King of Cups has a benign demeanor. He is a personality who brings a sensitive attitude to his work, his family, his relationships, and his community. If not representing an actual person, this card's appearance represents these qualities. At the symbolic level, this King represents a person who has deep feelings but is able to manage them because of concern for others, which is a major priority.

KEY WORDS FOR THE KING OF CUPS UPRIGHT

A wise counselor. A good father. A kindly authority figure. Maturity. Compassion. A mature, emotionally stable man. An artist or creative person, perhaps a teacher. A trusted advisor. A man in the helping professions. Someone you can rely on. Consideration. A good listener.

Upright

This King personifies a kindly man well disposed in a paternal manner toward you or the situation in question. He may represent your own father or a mature man in that role. If he is a person in your life, he is a "feeling type" who shows emotions easily and has strong family ties. As a parent, he will forgo his other desires to be with and care for his family. As a friend, advisor, or authority figure, you can be sure he is trustworthy and dependent. You can rely on his coming through for you. Rarely in a teen's reading does this King represent a romantic interest, unless there is an older man/young woman situation. However, his appearance can occasionally suggest a male love interest who is kindly, artistic, and mature for his age.

Reversed

When this King is reversed, he tells that it's time to move on from dependency on an older man—your father, a loved teacher, a familiar advice-giver—and strike out on your own. The old pattern with you as the young person looking up to your elders is outgrown, and you need to develop a sense of independence. Some children find it difficult to let go of the safety of parental advice and support. But in order for you to claim your own maturity, you must be able to let go of dependency. If this card represents your father, he may be more of a "good buddy" than a strong authority figure. This card can also signify someone who wants to get rid of you, someone who's trying to push you out of the nest.

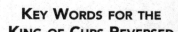

KEY WORDS FOR THE KING OF CUPS REVERSED

Difficulty with a mature man. Lack of trustworthiness. Need for independence from an absent or distant father. A man given to gambling or addictions. Insincerity. Selfishness. Bad money manager. Learning responsibility. Self-indulgent. Need for self-discipline.

QUEEN OF CUPS

People represented by the Queen of Cups tend to express their emotional, creative, and spiritual natures easily. Often they are artists, writers, poets, or psychics. They have a strong interest in the metaphysical world and may pass this on to their children. Such women bring out the best in others because they are concerned with the others' welfare. The sincerity of the Queen of Cups and her benign attitude draw people to her. She is known for grace, sweetness, patience, and unconditional love. As a parent, she is always sensitive to her children's feelings and needs.

KEY WORDS FOR THE QUEEN OF CUPS UPRIGHT

A nurturing woman. Emotional kindness. Imagination. Love of art. Musicality. Love of children. Quiet. Caring and loving. Mystical. Psychic ability. A homebody. Empathy. Occult learning or interest. Divination. Affection. A sixth sense. The heartstrings. Devotion. Goodness. Introspection.

Upright

The Queen of Cups is a benevolent, mature woman, full of grace and kindness. She represents an affectionate and loving woman who could be your mother, an older female relative, or a mature woman friend. Wise in the ways of love and the human heart, her attitude is one of receptiveness and approachability. She is creative, visionary, and psychic; but she tempers her intuitive ability with mature judgment. If she does not represent a person, the situation is likely to concern creative projects or circumstances with a positive maternal emotional tone.

Reversed

When reversed, this Queen can represent someone who is emotionally needy and demanding. She may be an alcoholic or an absent mother, someone who has mental problems or has had a breakdown. Or she may simply be a space case or an idealist who has never learned to function in the real world. As a negative mother figure, she is unresponsive to her children's needs or unable to fulfill them properly. She may turn her child into the parent, making the child responsible for her welfare. Emotional immaturity can be a problem with this type of woman, creating an unstable home life.

KEY WORDS FOR THE QUEEN OF CUPS REVERSED

Emotional instability. Spaciness. Alcoholism. Gullibility. Inattentiveness. Poor judgment. Bad management. Emotional outbursts. Negative thinking. Blaming others. Making demands. A phony psychic reader. Escapist. Daydreamer. Moody. Not grounded in reality. Unreliable. Fickle. Indecisive.

KNIGHT OF CUPS

The Knight of Cups is a romantic figure, portraying someone who is moving steadily toward his or her heart's desire, whether that is a course of study leading to a chosen career or a romantic attachment leading to marriage. This Knight is a symbol of loyalty and love, the ability to use intuition and creative imagination in everyday life. Representative of an older teen, this Knight indicates a sense of empowerment and understanding of the value of love and loyalty. His energy is often expressed by metaphysical or occult interests or study. He embodies generosity, sensitiveness, and caring for family, friends, animals, and the environment.

KEY WORDS FOR THE KNIGHT OF CUPS UPRIGHT

Love and romance. Messages about love. Love letters. Intimate communications. A dream come true. "Follow your bliss." Important emotional developments. A proposal of marriage. The arts. Dreams. Dancing. Music. Idealistic fantasies. Psychic ability. Imagination.

Upright

The Knight of Cups traditionally brings you a message about love entering your life. You may be deeply involved in a romantic situation that has all but taken over your life. He can bring a long-awaited message such as a declaration of love, an invitation to an important social event like your high school prom or homecoming, an engagement, or a proposal of marriage. You may feel this is *the* relationship you have been waiting for and dreaming about all your life. Just don't lose your head to your heart totally! If this card does not signify a love interest, it signifies a true friend, honest, intelligent, and helpful, someone you trust.

Reversed

This is a young person who likes to flirt and lead the other party on but is insincere and fickle, adhering to the "love 'em and leave 'em" attitude of love relationships. The love message you long for has been delayed or may never come. The romantic fulfillment you yearn for is superficial or based on deception or emotional shallowness on the other person's side. You could be hooked on someone whose feelings for you aren't very deep, who is just leading you on, or who will never make a commitment. It's time to cut your losses, lick your wounds, and move on.

PAGE OF CUPS.

PAGE OF CUPS

The Page of Cups represents a youth who is in the process of learning about the world, especially the world of feelings and love. The type of teenager portrayed by this page is sensitive, artistic, feeling-oriented, empathetic. He or she may also be a dreamer, impractical, unrealistic, immature. Such people are usually eager to please, softhearted, shy, reticent, open, and sincere. This card can indicate a pregnancy. Your mother may be having another child, or you or a friend or relative may be pregnant. Sometimes the pregnancy is unexpected or unplanned or presents a problem. If not a person, this Page indicates a situation that is in flux—blowing hot and cold and unpredictable.

KEY WORDS FOR THE PAGE OF CUPS UPRIGHT

Puberty. Emotional sensitivity. Love secrets. A pregnancy or birth. Artistic ability. News about love. Social activities. A young friend. Children. Gentleness. Kindness. A student. Pets. Tenderness. Emotional growth. Learning about love. Artistic sensibility. The inner child.

Upright

This Page is a young person who is bringing you a message about love. Or a message about love is coming somehow—via e-mail, letter, telephone, or in person. The situation might involve emotional risk, such as a secret engagement or elopement. Something is not quite as it should be. Circumstances around the message may be exciting yet scary at the same time. If the card represents you, the prediction is that you have already decided to take the risk and aren't interested in being persuaded otherwise. You are confident everything will work out. If this Page seems to represent someone who is quite young, it may be a warning to be on the lookout for an unwise emotional involvement.

Reversed

The Page reversed recommends that you be on guard in matters of love, especially communications about it. Someone inappropriate may be attempting to seduce you and you are unaware of the falseness of his or her intentions. This card represents a "fishy" situation that requires a careful assessment. For teens today, Internet romance is popular but chancy. Handle it with caution. You need to look clearly at all messages about love. If not a person, there may be a situation involving deceit, flattery for unsavory purposes, an unwanted pregnancy, or the keeping of dangerous secrets about love matters. If you are playing around with someone's emotions, take care—you might get hurt yourself.

KEY WORDS FOR THE PAGE OF CUPS REVERSED

Sorting out feelings. False promises of love. Seduction. What you see is not what you get. Insincere communications about love and romance. Beware of deceit. Don't give you heart casually. Watch out for trickery. Secrets can be dangerous. Don't fall for flattery.

ACE OF CUPS

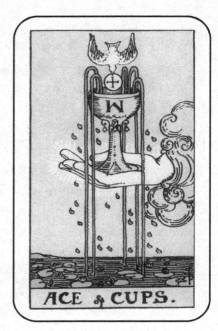

Upright

The Ace of Cups predicts a new love or a new beginning that promises harmony. For teenagers, it tells of new emotional experience, ability to express feelings easily, and a growing sense of personal identity. It points to positive interactions with others. If you are entering high school, you'll make friends easily and perhaps find a satisfying love relationship. There's also the promise of good health and positive emotional energy. The love it represents is pure and good, allowing you to open your heart fully. Your inner life will be enriched.

KEY WORDS FOR THE ACE OF CUPS UPRIGHT

New love. Harmonious new beginnings. Emotional well-being. Positive self-image. Pleasure. Joy. Good luck in love. Awakening of emotions. Idealistic imaginings. Being a feeling person. Firm sense of identity. An upsurge of emotion. Happiness. Falling in love. Tender feelings. Romance.

Reversed

When reversed, this Ace suggests mixed emotions, mood swings over love and romance, holding back feelings, or an inability to love because of inhibitions. There is disappointment in love or a new beginning that fizzles out. It takes a lot of effort to get anything new going right. Delays frustrate and drain you emotionally. Negative feelings are getting in your way regarding love matters, or you are constrained by circumstances about expressing your feelings. Look for the silver lining.

KEY WORDS FOR THE ACE OF CUPS REVERSED

"Love's labor's lost." Unrequited love. The end of an affair. Loneliness. Feeling isolated and unloved. Emotionally unfulfilled. Too shy to let others know how you feel. Unhappiness. Loss or separation from what you love. Tears. Recriminations. Loveless sex. Relationship problems. Grief.

Two of Cups

Upright

The Two of Cups symbolizes harmonious relationships of all kinds. You may be in the "honeymoon" stage of a romance that is mutually supportive and understanding. In a teen's reading, this card could indicate something as minor as a date or as important as an engagement. It could point to a new relationship or new harmony in an existing one. This card is also about making choices based on mutual needs, and about pleasing another person and setting aside selfish motives. Emotional expression is important, but it has to be honest and forthright to produce the needed cooperation.

Reversed

When reversed, choices may be more difficult, and there can be obstacles to love and harmony. A date may go sour, or you might be attracted to someone who doesn't return the interest. Shyness or not feeling good about yourself may keep you from letting another person know how you feel; or the romance may have to be kept a secret from disapproving parents. You want to make up with someone but are having difficulties. A friendship is under strain.

KEY WORDS FOR THE TWO OF CUPS UPRIGHT

A harmonious relationship. Cooperation. Mutuality. Sharing. Attraction. Romantic love fulfilled. A happy couple. Making friends. Ending strife. Getting along with others. Reconciliation. Finding common ground. A love affair. A partnership. Engagement. Marriage. Reciprocity. Compromise.

KEY WORDS FOR THE TWO OF CUPS REVERSED

Unrequited love. A relationship ending. Parting. Misunderstandings. Lack of cooperation. Need for secrecy in love matters. Disagreements. An unequal situation. Out of balance. Broken trust. Disharmony. Your ex-love. Complacency. A love gone wrong. Inability to discuss things openly.

KEY WORDS FOR THE THREE OF CUPS UPRIGHT

Celebrations. Good times. Parties. Social events. Happiness. Having fun. Getting together with friends. Enjoying holidays. Good feelings all around. Meeting new people. Excellent rapport with everyone. A circle of good friends. Family reunions. Everything's A-okay. Kindred spirits.

KEY WORDS FOR THE THREE OF CUPS REVERSED

Delays and disappointments about social events. A party postponed. Small celebrations. Lack of friends. Inability to find like-minded company. A romantic interlude ends. Refusal of permission to give a party. Expected company doesn't show up. Overindulgence. A social event is canceled.

Upright

Something has been completed. It's time for a celebration! You are experiencing victory and success, merriment and good times. You may be throwing a party to celebrate getting engaged or going steady, or attending parties that mark a happy occasion such as graduation or seasonal holidays. There are festivities, friendship, fun, and games. Whatever bad or murky feelings you previously had are gone and you are clearer now, with greater understanding of your emotional needs and those of others. You're on your way on a good road.

Reversed

The Three of Cups reversed isn't negative but only indicates that there will be delays and minor disappointments. A rainstorm might spoil an outdoor celebration, or a party is postponed because someone is under the weather. An invitation you hoped for may not arrive. You want to throw a party but can't spend the money just now. Everything's in a minor key. Happy occasions and celebrations will be smaller than you had hoped for.

FOUR OF CUPS

Upright

This card suggests a time of withdrawal from daily activities in order to go within. You need to spend time by yourself, drifting and dreaming, before returning to your hectic schedule of school, social activities, and extracurricular events. You may have been involved in an intense emotional situation, and now you have to withdraw to get proper perspective on it all. You need space in which to contemplate and sort things out. Feeling let down after a big buildup, you require some rest and recuperation. Learn to relax and let go of tensions.

KEY WORDS FOR THE FOUR OF CUPS UPRIGHT

Withdrawal from everyday concerns. Going within. Dissatisfaction with things as they are. Unmotivated. Needing rest and seclusion. Feeling misunderstood. Needing to make a decision. Being alone. Feeling empty.

Reversed

You are recovering from a period of discontent and dissatisfaction. You've gone within and spent some time alone and are now ready to emerge from your seclusion and get on with your life. You've got things to look forward to, such as social invitations and renewed interest in your projects. Now that the time of feeling "out of it" is ending, you are free to make new plans and carry out new creative projects for renewal.

KEY WORDS FOR THE FOUR OF CUPS REVERSED

Renewal. End of seclusion. Coming out of your shell. Accepting social invitations. New motivation. Satisfaction. End of discontent. A new perspective. New opportunities. Getting on with your life. Enjoyment.

KEY WORDS FOR THE FIVE OF CUPS UPRIGHT

Brooding over past losses. Fixated on what's wrong. Unable to see the forest for the trees. Emotional distress. Resentments. Maladjustment. Your glass is half empty. A love gone wrong. Regrets. Self-blame. Feeling bad about yourself. Pessimistic. Feeling sad or left out. Self-isolation.

KEY WORDS FOR THE FIVE OF CUPS REVERSED

A ray of hope. Acceptance. Looking toward the future. Optimism. Good news. Understanding the past. Recovery from loss and disappointment. Getting on with your life. Positive thinking. Making the best of a bad situation. Renewed hope for your future. Expecting the best. Opportunity.

FIVE OF CUPS

Upright

The Five of Cups symbolizes someone who is crying over spilt milk, focusing on a painful past and unwilling to look forward to a positive future. It's a case of perceiving the cup as half empty instead of as half full. In a word, pessimism. You're feeling that things will never get better. You're holding onto past disappointments, wrongs, losses, and hurt feelings. As the Five of Cups signifies inner change, it is a card of choice. You can continue to brood over what hurt you, or you can undergo attitude adjustment and begin to focus on what can go right in the future. You don't have to be miserable. You can make the effort to live in the present and let go of the past.

Reversed

When reversed, this Five suggests you are making appropriate changes in your inner self to rectify the situation. Your painful experiences are over now and you are on the way to recovery. You are willing to let bygones be bygones, to forgive and forget. An old love may be rekindled. You can accept that your emotional pain has served a purpose—you learned something valuable. You're willing to pick up the pieces and go on now.

Six of Cups

Upright

This card refers to a sentimental remembrance of things past, nostalgia, and good memories. You may be thinking of a happy childhood. During times of stress, pleasant memories are a comfort. Knowing you were happy in the past helps you to know how to be happy in the future. Issues surrounding your childhood are prominent, as your feelings connected to the past are going to affect your future. Or someone from your past has come back into your life, making you happy. Recreation and social pleasures are predicted, sometimes with old friends, or with family members.

KEY WORDS FOR THE SIX OF CUPS UPRIGHT

Childhood memories. Past happiness. Nostalgia for an idealized past. An old flame. The good old days. Remembrance of things past. Children. A family reunion. Birthdays. Anniversaries. Family gatherings. Emotional renewal. A family vacation. Togetherness. Siblings. Younger relatives.

Reversed

You are attempting to return to the past, which is over. You are wallowing in sentimental memories because of present difficulties, wishing for what once was. You may have a problem growing up and accepting responsibility, wanting to cling to childish ways and dependency. You may be quarreling with siblings or other family members. A past relationship may be troublesome. You have "inner child" issues.

KEY WORDS FOR THE SIX OF CUPS REVERSED

Gone but not forgotten. Clinging to the past. Refusal to grow up. Mired in memories. Family ties restricting your movement. Mommy's apron strings. Hanging on to outworn forms of security. Haunted by the past. Need to live in the present. Difficulty facing reality. Problem child.

KEY WORDS FOR THE SEVEN OF CUPS UPRIGHT

A multitude of choices. Imagination. Dreaminess. Many possibilities. Head in the clouds. Inability to decide. Unclear about objectives. Multi-talented. Too many options. Multiple goals. Determining a clear course. "Quo vadis?" Pulled in several directions. A hidden value.

Upright

The Seven of Cups signifies that you have many options—too many to make an easy choice. The problem is choosing what is best for you. You may be considering your future career or job aims, trying on first one idea and then another. This Seven points to fantasy and imagination, building castles in the air, emotionally exploring various possibilities. You may be scattering your energies in pursuit of first

one object of desire and then another, running around in circles, unable to make a committed choice. Your imagination is having a ball contemplating the huge variety of things you might like to do, while you are having a hard time making a decision.

KEY WORDS FOR THE SEVEN OF CUPS REVERSED

Decision making. Getting clear about what you want and can do. Feeling confident. Making the right choice. Letting go of unrealistic expectations. Having a realistic attitude. Goal-oriented. Clear-minded. A diligent student. Pursuing the right course. Making up your mind. Focusing.

Reversed

Things are beginning to come clear and you are nearing a choice among the multiple options available to you now. The fog is lifting, and you are better able to assess your choices; or you now have fewer options from which to choose. You are giving up wanting to have it all, buckling down to face reality. Your practical sense is coming forward to help you make the right decision. You aren't being lured by "pie-in-the-sky" promises or illusory ideas. You can meet your own expectations.

EIGHT OF CUPS

Upright

The Eight of Cups hints that the only solution to the present problem is to walk away from it—either physically or metaphorically—and go in another direction. Sometimes, what's happening is just that you are bored, stifled, or plain fed up. In an extreme case, a teenager might run away from home or go to live with the other parent if there's been a divorce. The Eight indicates a need for order and stability, emotional balance and serenity. However, when things just aren't working out as expected, it's often time to turn your back and leave. I certainly don't suggest becoming a runaway teen; but a safe change of residence might be the answer to a difficult living arrangement. How you handle the energy of this card will depend on your age and the severity of the problem.

KEY WORDS FOR THE EIGHT OF CUPS UPRIGHT

Getting away from it all. Moving forward alone. Breaking loose. A hermit. Leaving the past behind. Finding a new lifestyle. Going on a spiritual quest. Abandoning former ideas and opinions. Leaving home the first time. Relocating. Saying goodbye. Risking uncertainty. A wilderness trek.

Reversed

Reversed, this card has multiple meanings—you may be going on a short getaway vacation, returning to a more stable way of life, returning home after being away, settling down. You may have elected to remain in a relationship that is unsatisfying or uncommitted. You need to seek out new ways of dealing with what isn't working. Internal processes may be heightened as you cope with your problems. Someone may be leaving you.

KEY WORDS FOR THE EIGHT OF CUPS REVERSED

Refusal to leave. Not moving on. A static situation. Sticking it out for better or worse. Difficult endings. Returning to the fold. Social engagements. No time to be alone. Becoming more active. Getting things going.

Upright

KEY WORDS FOR THE NINE OF CUPS UPRIGHT

The wish card. Dreams come true. Fulfillment. Contentment. Good luck. Winning. Enjoyment. The world is your oyster. Physical pleasures. Happy romance. Untroubled times. Financial security. Getting what you desire. Luxury. A well-deserved holiday. Having a fairy godmother.

This is called the "wish card," for it shows all your dreams coming true. Getting it is like winning the lottery and falling madly in love all on the same day. You will have a time of fulfillment. Nobody ever has anything bad to say about this Nine. With it, you can expect everything you want and hope for (within reason!)—especially if it is in the outcome position. When the Nine of Cups appears ask, "What is my dearest wish?" However, remember the old adage: "Be careful what you wish for, you may get it." Nine represents gestation, so a birth or pregancy is possible, or a process requiring nine months for completion.

KEY WORDS FOR THE NINE OF CUPS REVERSED

Superficiality. Overindulgence. Not getting what you want, or not being happy with it when you get it. Greed. Emotional immaturity. Not knowing how to handle your luck. Being too materialistic. Stinginess. Working hard to make things happen. Being disappointed.

Reversed

Even reversed, the Nine of Cups isn't bad. You may squander money that came to you unexpectedly and regret it. Good luck may make you smug or think you are better than others less well off. You may abuse privileges. You may have wished for something you don't really want or need. There may be strings attached to extra money. Instant gratification may become a bad habit. You may indulge to excess and gain weight or get drunk.

TEN OF CUPS

Upright

The Ten of Cups is a wonderful card, symbolizing what most people want out of life—a fulfilling romance, love and harmony in the home, financial security. For a teen, this card represents emotional maturity and success at many levels. You are living in accord with your deepest self and reaping the spiritual rewards, as well as enjoying material well-being. You have good family relationships and value the support you get. Family celebrations are coming soon. Friendships are plentiful and rewarding. You feel a sense of belonging and empowerment. Whatever your question, all will turn out well, especially if this Ten is in the outcome position.

KEY WORDS FOR THE TEN OF CUPS UPRIGHT

Joyful times. Good things happen. A positive outcome. Emotional maturity. A happy family life. Friendship. Romance. A secure relationship. Bliss. Compatibility. Spiritual realization. A thankful celebration. Tranquility and peace. Coming home. Social activity. Getting together with friends.

Reversed

As this is such a positive card, the reversed position is not a difficult one. You may experience delays and obstacles to a cherished wish or project, or find someone standing in the way of your achieving your goals or the happiness you seek. Usually, the problem is external circumstances beyond your control. The only course of action is to do nothing until they change; and change they will. Keep a positive attitude and soon all will be well. You are in charge of how you respond to the situation.

KEY WORDS FOR THE TEN OF CUPS REVERSED

Delays. Obstacles. Disharmony. Discord. Conflict. Divided loyalties. Conflict of interest. Adolescent crisis. Delinquent behavior. Rebellious attitude. Quarreling in the family. Not getting ahead. Leaving home prematurely. Without family support or ties. Disruption in the family.

Tarot Play Exercise

GETTING TO KNOW THE CUPS

Here is the last round of this exercise that tests your knowledge of the pip cards while giving you practice relating the number cards to their meanings.

Separate the pip cards into the four suits. For this last round, you'll choose the Cups. Arrange them in numerical order, from Ace to Ten. Next, without referring to the meanings given in this chapter, examine the cards and see what you remember about each number's meanings. Use the illustrations on your deck to help you fix the meanings in your memory. (Remember, the pip cards are illustrated in most decks as an aid to memory.)

Now, in your Tarot notebook, list the numbers Ace through Ten under "Cups," and jot down whatever key words and phrases you remember, or any spontaneous ideas that pop up. When you're done, go back and check your list against the meanings given for the Cups pip cards.

13

Spreads for Readings

There are many ways to lay out a Tarot spread. Some spreads, like the Celtic Cross, are standardized and used widely. In fact, the Celtic Cross is usually the first spread taught to beginners. Although I will describe it later, I don't recommend it for students who are just starting out. For one thing, it requires ten cards. That's a lot to blend into a whole when you are just learning the meanings of the cards. For practice readings, I recommend using fewer cards. Also, a simple layout is best for asking specific questions. More complex layouts are for overview purposes or for long-term use.

There is one large spread requiring twelve cards that I do recommend you learn and practice with—the Horoscope spread. I will explain it later. This spread is good, especially for young readers, because each card represents an area of life that corresponds to one of the houses of an astrological chart. This is an easy spread to use for seeing the big picture, and if you're interested in astrology it is especially good.

A Cautionary Note

No one knows exactly how the Tarot works. Many have put forth theories to explain how shuffling a deck of cards and laying them out in a spread can give off such uncannily accurate information. Some believe that your unconscious mind directs the shuffling process, because, without being aware of it, at a deep level you already know the answers to your questions. Others think that an "invisible hand," such as a spirit guide, moves the cards into the positions in the deck. Still others cite the universal principle of synchronicity whereby meaningful coincidences create the impression of a sort of foreknowledge that is really a picture of the present moment. I don't claim to know the answer, nor do I believe anyone else does. What is clear is that the cards are connected with power. Therefore, it is important to recognize at the outset that you are dealing with power you cannot fully understand. Failure to respect that power absolutely can cause serious problems. Take my advice: approach the Tarot with seriousness, and never, never fool around with the cards for mere amusement or frivolous entertainment purposes.

For daily readings, which I especially recommend to students, choose a particular spread and stick with it. You can use any of the three-, five-, or seven-card spreads given in this chapter for your daily practice. Get used to one of these and become well acquainted with both the meanings of the cards and how you relate them to the whole reading before moving on to practice with a different spread. Your intuition will tell you when it's time to explore more complicated spreads. As you become more confident of your understanding of the multi-level meanings of the cards, you can vary the layouts by asking for clarification, using random cards from the deck.

You can also design your own spreads. As you become familiar with the spreads shown here, you'll begin to see how they work. Then you can use your imagination and the needs of the situation to create your own unique spreads. You may hit on one that suits you better than anything else. Use as many or as few cards as you like when designing your own spreads. You can revise standard spreads or use original spreads either for special purposes or as your own Tarot "signature." The possibilities are endless and fascinating. That's what is so wonderful about working with the Tarot!

The three- and five-card spreads are described in many books on the Tarot because they are basic layouts. The seven-card spread is my own invention. I have found it extremely useful not only for daily readings but for getting a reading started with a client. I call it the "Take Your Temperature" reading.

Important Note: Whichever spread or spreads you decide to use, be certain to record *all* your readings in your Tarot notebook. The simplest way is to draw the outline of the cards in the shape of the spread and then write the name of the card inside each outline. You can then jot down notes about your interpretation. If possible, do a verification as soon as possible. And don't forget to date your readings in your notebook for future reference.

Make notes about your day—what was going on, the weather, how you were feeling—if you were blue, moody, confused, happy, elated, optimistic, thoughtful—or just calm and neutral.

The Yes/No Draw

This is an easy way to get a quick answer to an immediate question. Simply decide in advance which cards will say Yes and which No. You can choose as you like, but here are some suggestions:

Major Arcana: Always yes if upright. Always no if reversed.

Minor Arcana: Even numbers = Yes. Odd numbers = No.

Court Cards: King = No. Queen = Yes. Knight = No. Page = Yes.

Note: If court cards are upright, the Yes or No is definite. If court cards are reversed, the Yes will be delayed; a No can be changed.

THE THREE-CARD SPREAD

This is the simplest, most basic spread, other than using a single card for a "yes/no" answer, or a three-card random-draw spread. It offers the flexibility of choosing in advance what each card placement will signify. These are the choices, going from left to right:

- Past, Present, Future

- Past major influence, Present major influence, Future major influence

- External circumstance, Present situation, Likely Outcome

- Immediate future, Near future, Distant future

- Yourself, Your present situation, Obstacle

- Body, Mind, Spirit

- Nature of the situation, Your attitude, Key element involved

As you work with the three-card spread using these variations, you will find yourself getting into the mode you have chosen. The chances are you will think up other variations on this most basic of spreads. Here is an example of a three-card reading I did for a teenage girl who was having boyfriend problems. I selected the last variation above as the focus for the reading.

Sarah feared that her boyfriend was losing interest in her. He seemed distant and didn't telephone very often. This upset her because she had thought the relationship was on a firm footing, yet she couldn't deny her feeling that something was wrong. She just didn't know what it was or what to do about it. She suspected he was interested in someone else, maybe seeing another girl. Here's what the Tarot told her:

For the nature of the situation, Card 1 turned up the Chariot. This indicated that Sarah was being pulled in two directions: her head said something was wrong, but her heart wanted it to be all right. The Chariot told her she had to get centered and not let her emotions get the best of her. To get at the truth of the situation, she needed to get her thoughts and emotions working in tandem.

In the attitude position, Card 2 was the Three of Swords. This revealed that she was already emotionally wounded and had lost trust in her boyfriend because of his suspicious behavior. When I questioned her, she admitted it wasn't the first time she'd felt like this, although before she had repressed her feelings because she didn't want the relationship to end. She was hurting, but separation was inevitable and she knew it.

For the key element to consider, Card 3 turned up the Eight of Cups. It showed she needed to move on. She was disappointed and unhappy with the current situation and needed to leave it behind so she could find a new love; to let go of what wasn't working and reflect on what she had learned from her suffering; to appreciate her new emotional maturity.

Sarah wanted to gain perspective on her relationship so I did another three-card spread for her using the first variation as the focus. Here's what came:

Card 1, in the position of the Past, was the Six of Cups, indicating that Sarah and her boyfriend had been happy in the innocence of a first love. Like children at play, they hadn't been aware of the fact that growing up can mean growing apart.

Card 2, in the position of the Present, was the Six of Swords, suggesting that Sarah was ready to leave the relationship, and leave her troubles behind her, which corroborated the first reading.

Card 3, in the position of the Future, was the Ace of Cups, which predicted that a new love was coming into her life soon.

THE SYMBOLIST LEGACY

The most far-reaching legacy of humanity's fascination with the use of symbols is the realization that the entire cosmos is suffused with *meaning*. Why is this significant? Because without meaning, life is empty, dull, flat, uninspired. When our lives lack meaning, we go off the rails, mess up, get in trouble, feel a deep sense of lack. But living life from a symbolist viewpoint turns the world into a realm of magic and mystery, proving that the physical world possesses a wealth of meaning beyond the merely material plane that we contact with our five senses. To use symbols as basic tools of life is to make a radical shift in the way we think about our world. It is to understand that life is a sacred text we can decipher through symbolic understanding.

THE FIVE-CARD SPREAD

This spread is especially good for practical advice. Another basic, often used spread, this adds two cards and enlarges the perspective. To do this simple spread, lay out the cards from left to right in a single row, the first card on the left being number 1. Here are the meanings of the positions:

1. Past influence

2. Present influence

3. Hidden influence

4. Advice

5. Likely outcome, if you take the advice given

Here is an example of a five-card spread, taken from a reading I did for a sixteen-year-old boy. John was in a state of indecision, and it was distracting him from his studies. A good student, he was going to graduate in a year, just after his seventeenth birthday. He'd always planned to attend college straight after graduation from high school; but the truth was, he was bored with school and impatient to get away from books and homework. Practical minded, he felt he was too young to take on the responsibility of a student loan and the workload of college life. He was considering taking off a year between high school and college to work, save some money for college expenses, and get some idea of how the world worked before choosing his college major and a future career. His parents were fully supportive of whatever choice he made.

Here's what the Tarot told him:

Card 1, in the "past influence" position, was the Ten of Wands, which said that he felt overburdened by his schoolwork, his sports and extracurricular activities, and having to hold down a part-time job. His family didn't have much money, so he'd have to pay for his college education himself. Already he worked a few hours a day after school in a fast-food restaurant, which left him little time for social activities. He just wasn't having any fun and wanted some time to catch up on what he'd been missing.

Card 2, in the "present influence" position, was the Ace of Wands, indicating he was eager to get on to something new. He wanted a real job, something satisfying that would advance his future career. This card promised the new beginning he was yearning for with the total focus of his present state of mind.

Card 3, in the "major influence" position, was the Eight of Pentacles, which indicated that he wanted to get to work earning money, even if in an entry position. He was preoccupied with the need for funds to pay for his education, but he also wanted practical experience in the real world of work, to acquire skills through on-the-job training.

Card 4, in the "advice" position, was the Fool. This card told him to follow his dreams, to take a leap into the unknown. He was being told to trust his instincts and the Universe. This could well be the most important decision of his young life, and he was advised to accept the challenge with an open heart. The Fool counseled him to get out and enjoy his youth, do what pleased him, before taking up the grind of studying for a career and settling down to a lifetime of work.

Card 5, in the "likely outcome" position, was the Sun, which predicted that all would be well. The sun would shine on his enterprise, he would be successful and happy. His thinking was clear, and he wasn't letting his decision be clouded by emotional turmoil. He was on solid ground and could rely on himself to make the right moves.

THE SEVEN-CARD "TAKE YOUR TEMPERATURE" SPREAD

As I said earlier, this one is my own invention, and I use it frequently. I always use it when doing readings for myself as a way of getting into the subject at hand. I also use a nine-card variation of this spread, which I'll explain later. To do this spread, first lay out one vertical row of three cards at the left-hand side of the spread, starting with Card 1 on the bottom; Card 2 above it; and Card 3, above that. Then place a single card, Card 4, to the right of Card 3. Next, make another vertical row of three cards on the right-hand side of the spread, with the top card as Card 5; beneath that, Card 6; and at the bottom, Card 7.

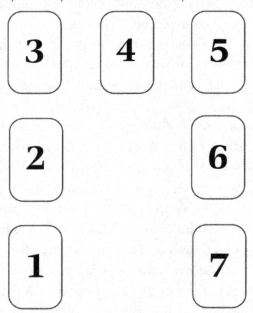

You can use this spread any way you like, assigning the positions as you choose. I vary what the positions will mean, depending on the querent and the question involved.

Here are the usual meanings I assign these positions:

1. The past influence

2. The present influence

3. The immediate future influence

4. What's uppermost on your mind

5. The obstacle

6. The helpful influence

7. The likely outcome

Here's an example of a reading I did for nineteen-year-old Margaret, who wanted to leave her home in Connecticut and move to Florida because she loved the beach and warm weather. Although she had spent a year attending a community college while still living at home, she wasn't sure whether she wanted to continue her education or get a job. Here's what the Tarot told her:

Card 1, in the position of the immediate past, was the Queen of Swords reversed, which represented her mother, a professional woman who tended to be emotionally distant and who wanted her daughter to finish college. Margaret had recently quarreled with her mother about her lack of academic ambition. Now she wanted to get away from her demands.

Card 2, in the position of the immediate present, was the Four of Wands, which expressed her concern over leaving her parental home and the security it offered. Margaret was somewhat timid and felt unsure about leaving her family and striking out on her own.

Card 3, in the position of the immediate future, was the Eight of Wands. This suggested that she would take a trip, probably by plane, which would help settle matters. I advised her to use her break time to go to Florida to see how she liked it and to check out job possibilities before making a final decision. She could even ask her mother to accompany her.

Card 4, in the position of what was uppermost in her mind, was the Five of Pentacles, representing her fear of not being able to make it on her own. Her family was well-off, and she had never wanted for anything material. But her mother held a tight rein on the purse strings and used money to manipulate her daughter, often telling her that if she left home she would starve. Now, Margaret was obsessed with the idea that she would be overcome financially by the demands of practical reality.

Card 5, in the external obstacle position, was the Moon. Margaret was very emotional, creative, dreamy, shy, and unworldly. She loved to write poetry and daydream. She knew she wasn't very practical, but she had a strong intuition and it told her that she needed to get away from her family and follow her dreams. I thought it interesting that Margaret wanted to live by the ocean—the Moon rules the tides. In the obstacle position, however, this card warned that Margaret needed to attend more to the practical side of life before she could make a move.

Card 6, in the position of the helpful influence, was the Queen of Pentacles, a mature woman with money and a good practical sense. When I asked Margaret if she could identify the card with a person in her life, she told me of her aunt, who was a businesswoman and very fond of Margaret. The aunt was sympathetic to Margaret's desire to be on her own and had already offered her financial assistance.

Card 7, in the position of the likely outcome, was the Sun. Could you ask for anything more? The Sun card in this position was a sure indication that she would be happy in a sunny climate! And that she would achieve success there. Moving to Florida, with her aunt's help, she would be freed of the sense of obligation she felt to her family and the awful guilt that was keeping her stuck and unhappy. This card clearly said, "Go for it! No fear!"

Variation on the "Take Your Temperature" Spread

After laying out the seven cards as described, draw two more at random from the deck. Put the first one in the center (beneath 4) and the second below that (in between 1 and 6). The center card is where your heart is, your "heart's desire," and the last card is the future that lies beyond the outcome or results from it. This is a useful way to get additional information. In the example given for Margaret, the center card was the Queen of Cups, confirming that Margaret wanted to be a mature woman but one who was creative and filled with inspiration. It turned out that she wanted to study art, to which her mother had objected on the grounds that it's difficult to earn a living as an artist. The last card was the Three of Pentacles, which predicted she could earn money if she learned her craft and practiced it well.

Verification

Margaret flew to Florida on her spring break and looked into art schools there. She found one with a work-study program that suited her needs exactly. Her aunt agreed to provide a monthly stipend to cover her expenses until she graduated. Seeing she was determined to follow her own course, her parents gave their blessing and were even glad to have a good excuse to visit Florida during the cold winter.

THE HOROSCOPE SPREAD

To lay out the horoscope spread, first choose a significator as previously described in chapter 5 and put it at the center of the spread. Then deal the cards from one to twelve and place them in a circle around the significator, laying them out counterclockwise.

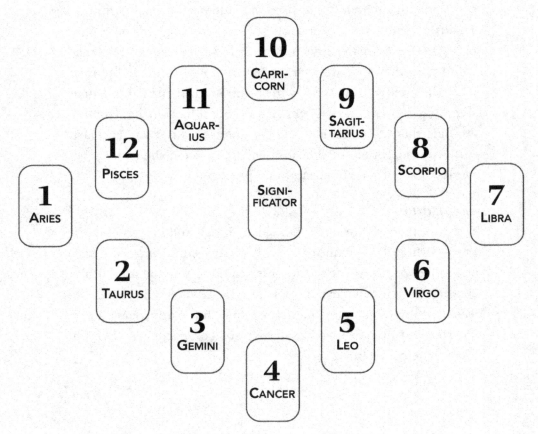

This spread is based on the twelve houses of the astrological chart. Each card represents the *area of life* designated by the house. To read this layout, begin with Card 1 for the first house, and interpret it accordingly. For example, the Sun appearing reversed in the first house would be an indication that the querent's usual sunny nature was being dimmed by the situation about which she is consulting the cards. She is experiencing personal stormy weather. Continue on around the circle in the same manner, putting together a story of the person's current life situation as you go.

Here are the basic domains of the twelve houses:

First House—The Self

The domain of the Self includes your sense of identity, physical characteristics, self-projection, the ego or "I am." That which is most personal to you. I-consciousness.

Second House—Personal Resources

The second house covers what you consider valuable, especially money and material goods, but also nonmaterial attributes. Also, your attitudes toward what you value.

Third House—Communications and Immediate Environment

This house relates to communications of all kinds—the stuff of daily life. It covers short-distance travel such as commuting. Also, siblings.

Fourth House—Foundation and Home

This represents the basic foundation of life, the Earth, our mother, and by extension the personal home and family, especially your own mother.

Fifth House—Creativity and Children

In the fifth house, we play, amuse ourselves, are self-expressive and creative. We encounter romance, love, and all kinds of affairs related to children.

Sixth House—Service Work and Health

This house is about your health and health care; for example, nutrition, hygiene, food preferences, daily routines. Also, service to others.

TEEN TAROT TIP
Must Read:
Teen Astrology

The Tarot and astrology go together like ham and eggs, like pizza and cheese. See my book *Teen Astrology* for a teen's-eye view of astrology and its relevance to you. In it you'll find such things as tables for you to look up your planets and their signs, information about the houses and how to place your planets in them, and how to get your chart free on the Internet—a neat idea.

When you have your own chart available and understand how it works, you can get a much richer reading from the horoscope spread, or from any spread, for that matter. I've covered the astrological correspondences between specific trump cards and the Signs and Planets in chapter 5 of this book.

Seventh House—Marriage and Partnerships

All one-on-one relationships fall here, not just marriage. These are *chosen* relationships involving mutuality and equality. Also, enemies.

Eighth House—Sex, Death, Other People's Resources

The house of Scorpio, this mysterious house relates to sex and death, and to other people's money, sometimes legacies. Also, the deep past.

Ninth House—Higher Mind, Long-distance Travel

The Ninth house refers to higher education, spiritual aspirations, and things foreign, including travel to faraway places. Also, freedom.

Tenth House—Social Status, Career

This house refers to our serious goals, social or professional status. It's about being in the world of action. It also represents the Father.

Eleventh House—Humanitarianism, Groups

This house symbolizes the world at large and our participation in it by way of groups, associations, clubs, societies, and community involvement.

Twelfth House—The Unseen

The last house is the domain of the deep inner Self, the unconscious, what is hidden. Also, solitude, confinement, secrets, incarceration, depression.

TEEN TAROT TIP
Clarification Cards

If at any time during a reading you find yourself puzzled, not quite able to grasp what a card is saying, ask for clarification by pulling out a single card at random and setting it beside the card you want to clarify. If you are still puzzled, draw a second card for clarification. Often this will give you a mini-three-card spread for that particular area of the reading, such as the future or the past, the outcome or the obstacle.

The Random-Draw Decision Spread

This is a quickie I invented for those times when you want a fast answer about a decision you're making and don't have the time to lay out your cards, or aren't in a place convenient for doing so. It's fast and easy. Just pull three cards from the deck at random (preferably after shuffling and cutting). If all three are Major Arcana, it's a good decision and you can make it with confidence. If one or more cards are Minor Arcana, you need to proceed cautiously. Court cards usually represent people affecting the decision and should be interpreted accordingly. If all three cards are pip cards, it's a bad decision and you need to think the matter through before taking action. Reading the meanings of each card will provide additional information.

TEEN TAROT TIP
Quick Mini-Relaxation Technique

Take a comfortable position, close your eyes, and tell yourself that you are now going to take ten deep breaths, and when you have finished you will be completely relaxed. Then, slowly and gently begin, counting off each deep breath. When you have inhaled/exhaled ten times, allow yourself to return to waking consciousness by breathing gently and easily, continuing to feel yourself being open to your inner possibilities. Write down what you felt and thought during the relaxation process for later reference.

For lots more information on relaxation exercises and how to use them effectively to access your inner knowledge, see my book *Your Psychic Potential*, pages 128–134.

THE TRADITIONAL CELTIC CROSS SPREAD

This spread always uses a significator. Put the significator in the middle of the table and place Card 1 on top of it. Place Card 2 crosswise on Card 1. Place Card 3 above, 4 below, 5 at the left side, 6 at the right side. Then lay Cards 7 through 10 in a vertical row at the right, with 7 at the bottom and 10 at the top. (See the diagram below.)

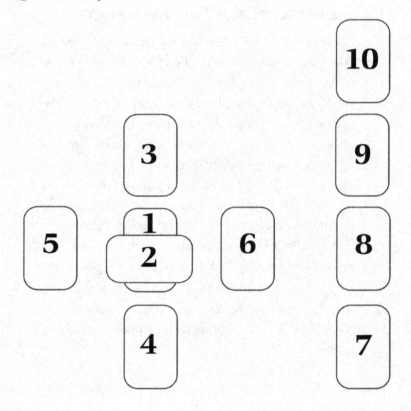

As you lay out the cards, say:

1. "This covers you." (Indicates the immediate concerns.)

2. "This crosses you." (The obstacles in force.)

3. "This crowns you." (What the querent knows.)

4. "This is beneath you." (Past influences.)

5. "This is behind you." (Distant past fading away.)

6. "This is before you." (New circumstances arriving.)

7. "This is your Self." (Querent's state of mind.)

8. "This is your House." (Surrounding circumstances.)

9. "This is what you hope or fear." (Wishes and fears.)

10. "This is what will come." (The likely outcome.)

As I've said, I rarely use this layout because I personally find it cumbersome and a bit long-winded. However, for complex questions it can be useful. Try it yourself—*after* you have become thoroughly acquainted with the simpler layouts—and see if you like it.

PRACTICE, PRACTICE, PRACTICE

The easiest and best way for beginners to learn to read the Tarot is to set aside some time each day to work with the cards. *Always* put yourself into a relaxed state, both mentally and physically, before using the cards. You can do this with simple deep breathing, by saying a prayer or a blessing, or by sitting quietly and "tuning in" for a few minutes. These are all good practices. Avoid reading the cards when you are upset or in an agitated state, for that will influence the reading. If you're disturbed, wait until you feel calm before consulting the Tarot. You need a clear mind to get a clear channel of communication.

Your relaxed state should include an expectation of success and a sense of optimism that the reading will provide valuable information regarding the question you are asking. Remember that the interpretations here or in any other book are not carved in marble. You are free to use your intuition and call on your imagination.

At first, your impressions will vary from apparently nonsensical to profound, and everything in between. No matter how you respond, take notes in your journal. When you review it, new significance will be revealed.

If a particular card seems especially significant, keep it out of the deck and look at it during the day, noting any new or different thoughts and feelings it provokes in you. Jot these down in your journal. Before retiring, compare the card with your notes about it. If you have a dream or fantasy related to the images on the card, write this down too. Dreams often comment on the daily work of study and reading.

Compare your readings of the same card on different dates to see if, and how, your interpretations have changed. Your personal hands-on experience with the cards will form the foundation for the meanings. When you start using more complex spreads, you will be giving your intuition a workout.

If you get poor results, you may not be in the right frame of mind or spirit. Concentrate on relaxation exercises beforehand. Sometimes, the channel just isn't clear. Do not let this deter you. Whenever you are learning a new skill, you will make mistakes, like hitting a wrong note while practicing a new piano piece. Just keep practicing regularly; before long, you will have it down pat.

READING FOR OTHERS

If you expand your Tarot use to reading for others, consider these sessions as *practice*, until you have gained considerable experience over time. Study of the Tarot is a lifelong process: there is always something new to learn, and the development of intuition is ongoing. It's not like you just memorize it as you did the multiplication tables and that's that. You have to spend both time and energy and get loads of practice before you are qualified to read for others. However, as long as you acknowledge to yourself and the person for whom you are reading that you are a novice and that your readings for others are strictly practice, feel free to do them. In the beginning, it is best to stick to people you know well, such as family and friends whose general situations you already know. You'll have the advantage of prior knowledge about the situation that is the subject of the reading. In such cases, a reading can confirm what a person only suspected, provide guidance in a difficult situation, or affirm positive conditions.

The best way to start a reading for someone else is to conduct an interview to find out what the person wants the reading to deal with. That way, knowing in advance the purpose and question, you can judge your interpretations accordingly. Sometimes it happens—quite often in my experience—that the cards won't seem to answer the question but will point to another concern, usually deeper, showing what's really on the person's mind. In these cases, the initial question is simply a screen for the real issue.

"Psychologists have hitherto failed to realize that imagination is a necessary ingredient of perception itself."

Immanuel Kant,
Critique of Pure Reason

When doing readings for others, be wary of doing predictions (fortune-telling). Remember that there are many variables in the psychic world, as life is never static. Today's situation may change by tomorrow. This is especially key advice when negative cards come up. It is safest to think in terms of *possibilities*, rather than making absolute statements about the future. If you make a definite statement of future ill fortune, you run the risk of creating a self-fulfilling prophecy. Instead, say something like, "It appears there might be a person around you who can't be trusted. Does that bring anyone to mind?" or "It's my impression you are experiencing anxiety and pain."

Let the person give you feedback, and if he or she doesn't confirm your interpretation, don't push it. The person may not be able to relate to or accept a negative interpretation, even if it is correct—and you cannot know (unless you are already in that person's confidence) whether or not it *is* correct without confirmation. *Always take great care choosing your words when you read*

Choosing Your Words

Although the Tarot, among the various divinatory methods that range from tea-leaf reading through astrology, is considered "high data/low subjectivity," the words you choose for interpretations are of vital importance. I can't stress their importance enough. We all know how words—even spoken in jest—can hurt, or how much an encouraging word can boost us up out of a bad mood. So, keep in mind that even in the case of Tarot, which is a data-rich system, your personal intuition is of prime importance. Always think before you speak, because the symbolic nature of the information the cards give you lends itself to various interpretations.

Of course, if you are reading for yourself and making notes in a Tarot journal, it's okay to write down the first thing that comes to mind. Later, review your interpretations and look at the cards again to see if they suggest other ideas or ways of expressing what you felt. Never be afraid to revise an interpretation in the light of new information. Remember, life is change.

for others. Even if it's a close friend, you can't know for sure the other person's inner state of mind or level of psychological savvy.

When reading for others on serious matters, be prepared for emotional responses. The Tarot has a way of reaching down deep when you aren't expecting it. In my years of doing readings, I've seen people become upset or agitated when the reading touched a sore point. As they recognize the truth of the reading, people often have tears in their eyes or even burst out crying. I always keep a box of tissues on my reading table. If a person's response is tearful, it's your job to reassure him or her that crying is okay and helps with healing. Many people repress tears because they feel embarrassed or guilty. They need you to provide reassurance. When you read for others, remember that you take on important responsibilities: one is to give aid and comfort, another is to be totally honest within the limitations of your interpretative skills. That's why hard-and-fast predictions are not advised. It's best to always allow some leeway and explain that there are many possible interpretations. If a situation is difficult or painful, draw clarification cards to show that things will get better.

Most often, however, you won't be addressing really serious matters. You'll be doing your practice readings for your friends and family on matters of relatively small importance, such as whether they should accept a blind date, attend a social event, pass an exam, deal with a sibling or parent, buy something they want, or go on a vacation. This by no means violates the general rule of being serious and respecting the power of the cards. Always be sincere, no matter how lighthearted the question, and don't ever use the Tarot to get yourself an ego boost. And remember that more serious issues may lurk underneath minor questions, which the Tarot cards will reveal.

Personal ethics are essential to the reading process. This cannot be overemphasized. If you choose to read for other people, you voluntarily accept responsibility for your interpretations. Should you feel at all unsure about how to interpret a card, you must be up-front with the other person. *Never, ever try to fake it.* When in doubt, say something like, "It seems that thus-and-such may happen, but I'm not getting this clearly." Do not hesitate to admit that you don't know everything, or that the flow of intuitive information is blocked or unclear. You are *practicing* and *learning,* a novice, not a professional. Take extreme care when you provide information to others. Never make absolute pronouncements, especially of the predictive type. Choose your words carefully to keep readings as clear and simple as possible. Don't use esoteric references or high-flown metaphysical explanations, no matter how much you may have read on these subjects. Never confuse the person by using unfamiliar technical terms. Stick to plain language, offering your insights with the other's needs in mind. A reading is only valid if you provide useful information or a new perspective. It's great to be "right on" but it's also very possible to be off-target.

After twenty years practicing the Tarot professionally, I never fail to determine a client's state of mind before a reading. On occasion, I have given the client back the fee because something was blocking the flow of information (usually the client being closed off)—the cards just weren't "speaking" to me. Successful readings for others require a state of rapport between the participants. The querent must be open to accept the information, and the reader must acknowledge being nothing more than a *channel* for knowledge transmitted from a Higher Source. The Source is always there, always available. It's up to those of us who practice the Tarot to learn how to access it accurately.

Go thou and do likewise!

The Emerald Tablet

"True, without error, certain and most true; that which is above is as that which is below, and that which is below is that which is above, for the performing of the miracle of the One Thing (or One Substance); and as all things were from one, by the meditation of one, so all things arose from this one thing by adaptation; the father of it is the Sun, the mother of it is the Moon; the wind carries it in its belly; the nurse thereof is the Earth. This is the father of all perfection, or consummation of the whole world. The power of it is integral, if it be turned into earth. Thou shalt separate the earth from the fire, the subtle from the gross, gently with much sagacity; it ascends from earth to heaven, and again descends to earth; and receives the strength of the superiors and of the inferiors—so thou hast the glory of the whole world; therefore let all obscurity flee before thee."

Attributed to the Greek sage Hermes Trismegistus

BOOKS OF RELATED INTEREST

The Way of Tarot
The Spiritual Teacher in the Cards
by Alejandro Jodorowsky and Marianne Costa

Teen Astrology
The Ultimate Guide to Making Your Life Your Own
by M. J. Abadie

Teen Dream Power
Unlock the Meaning of Your Dreams
by M. J. Abadie

Teen Psychic
Exploring Your Intuitive Spiritual Powers
by Julie Tallard Johnson

Spiritual Journaling
Writing Your Way to Independence
by Julie Tallard Johnson

I Ching for Teens
Take Charge of Your Destiny with the Ancient Chinese Oracle
by Julie Tallard Johnson

The Thundering Years
Rituals and Sacred Wisdom for Teens
by Julie Tallard Johnson

Teen Feng Shui
Design Your Space, Design Your Life
by Susan Levitt

Inner Traditions • Bear & Company
P.O. Box 388
Rochester, VT 05767
1-800-246-8648
www.InnerTraditions.com

Or contact your local bookseller